Understanding the Trinity

Also by J. P. Arendzen
from Sophia Institute Press®:

Ten Minutes a Day to Heaven

J. P. Arendzen

Understanding the Trinity

SOPHIA INSTITUTE PRESS®
Manchester, New Hampshire

Understanding the Trinity was originally published in 1937 by Sheed and Ward, London, under the title *The Holy Trinity*. This 2004 edition by Sophia Institute Press® contains minor editorial revisions to the original text.

Sophia Institute Press®
Box 5284, Manchester, NH 03108
1-800-888-9344
www.sophiainstitute.com

Nihil obstat: H. E. Calnan, *Censor Deputatus*
Imprimatur: Can. S. Banfi, *Vicar Generalis*
Southwarci, January 19, 1937

Library of Congress Cataloging-in-Publication Data

Arendzen, J. P. (John Peter), b. 1873.
   Understanding the Trinity / J.P. Arendzen.
      p. cm.
   Rev. ed. of: The Holy Trinity.
   ISBN 1-928832-15-6 (pbk. : alk. paper)
   1. Trinity. I. Arendzen, J. P. (John Peter), b. 1873.
Holy Trinity. II. Title.
BT111.3.A7 2004
231'.044 — dc22   2004016820

04 05 06 07 08 09 10 9 8 7 6 5 4 3 2 1

꙰

Contents

❧
Appendix

❧

Preface

In this treatise an attempt has been made to write about the mystery of the Blessed Trinity in a nontechnical way. It is obviously impossible to make such a treatise popular in the usual sense of the word, but the treatment might be made less forbidding to the laity than it often is. It seemed worth trying even to make it devotional in the sense of bringing out its beauty and attractiveness, the marvel and the grandeur of its truth. The author is keenly conscious of the imperfections of his own treatment, and yet hopes that with all its shortcomings, it might be a help to some to give more glory to the Father, to the Son, and to the Holy Spirit.

J. P. Arendzen
January 1, 1937

Editor's note: The biblical quotations in the following pages are taken from the Douay-Rheims edition of the Old and New Testaments. Where applicable, quotations have been cross-referenced with the differing names and enumeration in the Revised Standard Version, using the following symbol: (RSV =).

Understanding the Trinity

Chapter One

ᚚ

God invites you to
divine intimacy with Him

From the earliest ages, wise men have puzzled over the problem of the "One and the Many."

This world displays a wonderful variety and multiplicity of things to the wistful eye of man. Myriad objects affect his senses; countless substances and beings surround him. Although at first overwhelmed by their seemingly endless number, man never despaired somehow to reduce this manifoldness to some kind of coherence. And coherence means unity, some principle and power essentially one and undivided, from which all plurality descends.

A small section of mankind has completely lost its way in the search for the final unity underlying bewildering diversity. They went astray into the dreamland of pantheism. They sought the center of this far-flung universe within this universe itself. The Many were not really many; they were the One. The manifold world, perceptible to the senses, was only a phantom, they said, an illusion; the ultimate Reality was one Being which manifested or unfolded Himself in these endless phenomena, this shoreless sea ever-moving. *Phenomena* is but the Greek for "things that seem," "things that appear," but "the Thing underneath," was the one and only Thing that really existed; all things else were but a passing show. They were but the flickering, dancing lights on the bosom of the ocean. They were but the sheen of the billows, and the billows were the ocean itself and had no existence apart from its fathomless waters. Even men themselves, they maintained, were deceived in their individuality, their contrast between "I" and "Thou," for in the very depth of reality, "I" and "Thou" were the same, and selfhood was the deceitful glow and phosphorescence of an *ignis fatuus*. The supreme wisdom of man consisted in realizing that All was One and One was All and to recognize in his ego the Infinite One, the Absolute, and say, "I am All, and All is I."

Thus, in his feverish search for the One in the Many, man's brain became palsied, and denying the stark reality of the distinctness of things in him and around him, he stared as with the glassy eyes of the sick on the imagined spot of light, which to him became the whole of all that is, and he fancied he saw the totality of the universe in a mathematical point.

This mental disease has afflicted and still afflicts many, and great numbers are under the influence of soporific pantheism, but happily man in the mass is too sound and sane to forget the difference between himself and his neighbor or to imagine himself one with the rock or with the lichen upon it, or to think that he is his dog and his dog is he.

Common sense acknowledged the multifarious abundance of distinct objects in this varied world, but found the unity in the cause that produced them. Men found a transcendental unity above and beyond the visible world in the one Being which, with creative power, called this universe into being, as a multiple reflection of His own undivided, infinite glory. As a cunning workman or an inventive artist might produce a profusion of widely varying objects and yet not lose his own individuality, the indivisible unity of his own personality, so God, utterly one in Himself, could produce this myriad-fold world without losing the unity of His nature.

Only in this sense are all things one: that they are made by One; and being made by One, they all show forth the mind of the One, however varied among themselves they may be.

Nor, having created them, does that One leave them, but maintains them in being and thus continually impresses the unity of His mind upon them. All human science is but an endeavor to think once more the Thought that once made the world and now holds it in being. True science does not foolishly deny the multitude of distinct creatures, but reduces to ever higher unity the powers and laws that keep it and rule it.

God, who is the One, infinite in power and wisdom, conceived, planned, designed, and executed this intricate scheme of the great created *all* that we men style the universe in its vastness and multiplicity. But the finite, however large, does not exhaust the Infinite. The Infinite can dwell in the finite, but cannot be contained by it. The Infinite can hold the finite, but cannot be held by it. It can possess and pervade it, but not be possessed by it. God remains the infinitely Transcendent, although He is present within all that He has made.

So far, then, human reason can pursue the trace of the Eternal and demonstrate that beyond, and yet within, the Many there lies the One, who is cause of the Many and who, in creating the Many, yet never lost divine unity, existing without parts or divisions in the oneness of divine nature.

Having refused the opium of pantheism and the delirium of its dreams, rational man in the sobriety of wakeful thought stands before God, his Maker and the Maker of all that is. He has found the One in the Many and kneels to adore. He acknowledges the Infinite, the Everlasting, the Undivided, the only One, without a second, "the Father of lights in whom there is no change, nor shadow of alteration."[1]

He gazes on the almost blinding Sun, whose rays are scintillating on the wide ocean of created being and whose rays give them existence and substance. For they *are* because He shines upon them. They are the outcome of His *"Fiat lux,"* uttered in the beginning.

But man is daring. He has found the One, but he is not yet satisfied. This One is not a soulless thing. Greek philosophers may have designated the One by a neutral numeral, and have spoken of *to en*, that is, the one *thing*; and modern Germans may have echoed it by *das eine*, but man is not satisfied. He would love to discern something in that blank disk of dazzling light divine. He knows indeed

---

[1] James 1:17.

that it is not subject to fitful change. In that sense, nothing new can happen within it; it cannot be stimulated into successive activity by something that was not there before. Only the imperfect, only the limited, only what is divided in itself thus proceeds to action.

Man knows all that, and yet? Man can, of course, praise God as the Creator. Man can survey all that God has made and praise Him for having made it: the starry firmament and the expanse of ocean, the restless clouds and the cataracts of the waters. He can praise God for having set the mountains in their places and fixed the boundaries of the sea. Man can, like the psalmist, call upon the hoarfrost of winter and the freshness of spring to praise the Author of nature. He may bid the birds in the air and the beasts of the field to join man in giving glory to the Creator. Every blade of grass and every blossom on every tree may be cited to sing the bounty of God and to proclaim by their beauty the beauty of God. All life on earth must bear some likeness to the life of the One who made it. Any picture in some way reveals its painter, yet not all pictures are portraits, and even were they so, no colored canvas adequately reproduces the soul itself and the life of man. So it is with nature.

All nature tells of God, yet nature's life is not God's life. It is only an analogy and infinitely different. Man would love to know about God Himself, and not from others in feeble accents and distant parables, but from God Himself.

No doubt men learn more of God by His divine providence toward them than by the contemplation of nature around them. Israel knew more of God than the pagan, for it was God who led Israel out of Egypt and led them through the desert by a lightsome cloud. God spoke to them from the height of Sinai, God saw them safe into the land of promise, God defended them against their enemies, and God punished them when they went and worshiped the idols of the Gentiles.

Thus, God revealed both His justice and His goodness toward them, yet what God does, even to His intellectual creatures is, after all, not God's own inner sanctuary of the Godhead. Had God never created this world nor ever chosen Israel, He would still be God, dwelling in inaccessible heights of His own divine life. God was not bestirring Himself after an eternity of inactivity when He created the world. God is always life and therefore is always acting.

What, then, did God do before the world was made? What does God do within His own Godhead even now, since creating and maintaining worlds does not affect His inner life?

Understanding the Trinity

God is life; God is power in ceaseless activity. Now, life and act are to us men incomprehensible unless linked to some kind of duality or multiplicity, a going out and a reaching an end; if you like, a striving and an obtaining, a tending toward another and a grasping and embracing it. A life that is stillness absolute; a life in which nothing happens at all, nothing whatsoever, which remains the utter undifferentiated sameness of the One; a life in which there is no otherness at all is beyond our understanding and seems to involve a contradiction. An act that has no source and has no aim, an act in which the doer is utterly identical with the thing done under every conceivable aspect — how is it an act and not the stillness of stark immobility? If God lives, what is happening within Him?

We men are spirits, although possessed of a material body. Our highest life is that of thought and will. God made us; hence God, too, must have thought and will, for He could not have given us what He Himself does not possess. Divine thought and will are higher in kind by infinite projection and analogical proportion to ours, yet they must in some way be in God. If God thinks, what does He think? If God wills, what does He will? How is thought conceivable without some duality, under some aspect at least, of the thinker and the thought. How is will conceivable without some duality under some aspect of Him who wills and the object of His will? Yet God is one! But it is a unity that lives — a life that involves no change and yet is life.

It is as certain that God does not change as that God is one. The thing that changes is not yet that into which it changes and therefore not the fullness of infinite being; it is but an imperfect creature in the process of becoming or of development. God is not such. To explain God's life by change, change within from one state to another — that would be stark folly. Yet God lives. He thinks, and He wills. Thinking is an act of knowledge, but is knowledge possible without some duality in some way between knower and known? God wills. That means He loves, yet how is love possible without some duality between lover and beloved? Yet God is one. Who shall reconcile His life with His unity? Who can solve the riddle of the living God?

What are the events of Thy eternal life, O God, and who can tell the story of Thy inner self?

Besides Christianity, there are two world religions that proclaim the unity of God. The Jews' most sacred formula is "Hear, Israel, thy God is one God!" The Moslem cries from a thousand minarets, *"La Illah ila' lah!"* No god but

God! Great indeed is the truth of their faith, but they have no further proclamation to make. In the Synagogue they will praise God for having led them out of Egypt; in the Mosque they will say the *Fatha* to "the merciful and the compassionate" *Errahman, Errahim;* but beyond that they have no message about God. There is for them no revelation of God's own inner life. What God has done *for* them they know, but He has remained a veiled Majesty who has been bountiful indeed, but has not admitted them to sacred intimacy and told them about Himself, what goes on within the sanctuary of the Godhead. Or rather, He *has* told them, but they will not believe it.

And the pity of it! Even among those who are nomi-nally Christian, among those once baptized in the name of the Father and of the Son and of the Holy Spirit, there are some who refuse to believe that God has revealed His own life to the children of men. There are many more who, without refusing belief, yet look upon God's self-revelation as an encumbrance and a burden on a man's faith, as a piece of theology to be accepted merely as a trial to a man's intellectual submission and with no further purpose whatever; in fact, a useless mystification.

They do not see the loving kindness; they do not un-derstand the tender condescension of God in allowing us

God invites you to divine intimacy with Him

to know of His inner life in the temple of His divinity. We men are slow enough in admitting our fellowmen to the intimacy of our soul. We show them the outside, but not many are permitted to see the innermost truth about us as we ourselves know it. Only the dearest friends are invited to enter into the secrecy of our mind and will. We zealously guard the full reality against all intruders; only in close confidence do we allow our bosom friends sometimes to see us as we are, when all veils are drawn away.

When God, who had stood aloof from sinful mankind for many generations, at last came to redeem mankind and made them again His darling children, He bethought Himself and admitted them to the secrets of His divine intimacy. He revealed that within the Godhead there were three divine Persons, that there was the Father and His Son and the Love between them both, breathed out in holiness.

Even in the fierce light of the sun of His divinity, God allowed us to discern a Trinity, so that we might adore God, not merely for what He had done for us, but what He was in Himself.

True, He did not allow us to fathom the mystery, to plumb the depths of His infinite being, but He told us the truth as far as mortal mind can understand. He spoke to us about Himself as only a friend dares speak to a friend.

Chapter Two

ℳ

There are three Persons in one God

This is the sum of what is revealed:

There exist three divine Persons — Father, Son, and Holy Spirit — and these three Persons are really distinct, the one from the other.

Father, Son, and Holy Spirit are not just three aspects of the Divinity, or qualities, or just facets of the infinite truth, which in reality coincide, but seem only Three to us. They are not just modes or attitudes in which God manifests Himself to the outside world, appearing distinct to finite beholders, but identical in themselves. They are not merely names for God, as He reveals Himself in His dealings with us, as our Creator, Redeemer, and Sanctifier.

No, the Father is not the Son; and neither the Father nor the Son is the Holy Spirit. They are distinct among themselves, by a distinction as deep as their infinite nature. For all that, the Three subsist in one, numerically one, divine nature and Godhead, for there is only one God.

Three mere human persons share, of course, the same human nature, but this sameness is only generic; it is only a sameness of *kind*, not an identity of number. One single human being is not at the same time Peter, James, and John. Peter, James, and John are distinct one from the other not only in person, but in the totality of their being, for they are not numerically the same one, individual manhood. Humanity can be numerically multiplied, but divinity cannot. There is but one, single, undivided God, and this one infinite Reality, which is essentially alone, self-contained, and has no partner, this God is Father, Son, and Holy Spirit. God is thus one in nature, but three in Persons.

Furthermore, it stands revealed that, although these Three are utterly equal to one another with an equality that is absolute, since each of them is the same God, yet they are so far from being identical with one another that they are related to one another as relative terms in direct opposition, and their opposition lies in their relation of origin, the one to the other. The Father is distinct from the Son, because He eternally begets Him. The Son is distinct from the Father because He is eternally being begotten by Him. The Holy Spirit is distinct from both Father and Son, because He is breathed from both and proceeds from them as from one principle of origin.

So far the bald statement and bare outline of revealed truth.

Before we study it and establish its truth in detail, we must be quite clear what we mean by the terms *person* and *nature* when applied to God.

What, then, roughly speaking, is a person? It is some single subject, existing by itself — as this one complete thing in some order of being — and as the principle that acts and to which all actions and experiences are attributed as center of *responsibility*.

It is therefore an individual possessed of an intelligent nature. A man is a person, but a dog is not, because a man has intellect, and a dog has not. We might possibly call a dog an individual but not a person. The word *person* is reserved for an individual who is rational. A person, then, is essentially something utterly single and unshared. It may be possible to share qualities and attributes, but not to share personality, for its very notion demands singleness; a person designates essentially "this one and not another." A person is essentially a thing complete and subsisting by itself; the moment it is only part of another thing needed for the completion of itself, it is no person, but only an element of something else. All this is plain common sense; unaided human reason can see it and needs no revelation for its acceptance.

But revelation has come and widened and perfected our notion of personality, for it teaches us that in the one divine nature there are three persons, and that in Christ there are two natures, and only one person. Thereby we learn that the divine nature, although it is one single being, one individual substance and infinite intelligence, utterly complete in itself and unshared, it is yet not a person, for it is identified with *three Persons*, who are utterly distinct among themselves.

We learn, moreover, that Christ's human nature, even though it is this concrete, single, rational, individual thing, complete of its own kind, is yet not a person, but subsists in the infinite Person of God the Son.

In the Trinity, is the divine nature really objectively distinct from the three Persons? No, it is not. The Godhead *is* the three Persons.

Is, then, at least in each Person His nature not really distinct from His personality? In us indeed, person and nature are really distinct, for that by which I am a man is not that by which I am John and not Tom. Is this so in God? No. There is no *real, objective* distinction between the Father and the Godhead, nor between the Son or the Spirit and the Godhead.

What do we mean by that?

We mean that the most simple and transcendent reality of the divine Being objectively corresponds *both* to the reality of "nature" and the reality of "personality," so that in its uttermost simplicity, it is equivalent both to the reality of "essence or nature" and to the reality of the three Persons. In its simplicity, it verifies both concepts and it holds all that both realities would hold, even if they were distinct, which as a matter of fact they are not. If we realize this virtual distinction, we see that the nature and the three Persons are — and each Person is — in fact one thing in God, but they are thus in a way *as if* nature and persons were distinct. Such a distinction is therefore not purely a fiction of our brain without any ground or base in reality, a mere pretense for the sake of logical classification, but it is based on the real fact of the distinction between Father and Son, between the first Two and the third Person.

In order to see a little more clearly what this "virtual" distinction really involves and means, let us remember that there is a similar distinction between God's essence and God's attributes.

God is immense, all-pervading, just, wise, and merciful. Now, to us, immensity, omnipresence, justice, wisdom, and mercy are not the same things; they signify different, distinct qualities, and as qualities they can never be identical the one with the other. But in God there is no composition of any kind, not even the composition of substance and qualities. God is that one supereminent Reality that is utterly simple without any composition. He is mercy, might, justice, and wisdom all in one. He is that higher transcendent Being who, in His own indivisible simpleness, includes all the qualities that in created things are distinct among themselves and distinct from the substance of the thing in which they inhere. Yet when we men distinguish between God and His attributes and between mercy, justice, wisdom, and so on, our distinguishing is not an idle, groundless procedure, for it has a root in fact: the fact that what we understand by the quality of mercy is not what we understand by justice or wisdom.

In a somewhat similar way, we men are forced to distinguish between God the Father as person and His divine nature, the Son as person and His divine nature, and the Spirit and His divine nature, although in fact there is no such distinction in the realm of divine reality. There is, however, this difference between the case of the Trinity and the case of the divine attributes: in the case of the attributes, they are in God identical; in the case of the Trinity, the three Persons are infinitely distinct even in the Godhead, even though each Person is identical with the divine nature.

We conclude that we must give a somewhat sharper definition of *person* and say that it is indeed a single and complete rational substance, but we must add "wholly contained within itself," that is, not possessed by three as is the divine nature, and not receiving actuality from someone else, as the human nature of Christ.

Just now we used the word *substance*. In many ways, it is an unfortunate word, for when we use it, we almost irresistibly think forthwith of a concrete *nature* as such, a thing with its nature and individuality together. The word does not emphasize the person as distinct from the nature. Hence, for the sake of convenience, theologians have coined a word that is better and more characteristic. They speak of a person as a *subsistency* in a rational nature. Each divine Person, then, is a distinct subsistency in the one Godhead, or it might be better to say, not *in*, but *of* the one Godhead, lest anyone's imagination run away with him and fancy that each person was *part of* the divinity, and possessed each one-third of the whole nature of God. In truth the one indivisible God subsists thrice, that is, in the Father and the Son and the Holy Spirit.

How could this be said in simpler language?

Perhaps this way.

Nature answers the question "What is it?" *Person* answers the question "Who is it?" We are all aware of the distinction; it is sheer common sense and primary experience. We need no deep philosophy to know it; it comes spontaneously to our human reason. I am a person not because I am a man, for there are other men, who are just as much man as I am, yet they are not I. Hence, I am I, that is, I am a person, by another factor and principle of reality, which personalizes or individualizes my rational nature. If we apply this to God and could in childlike simplicity ask the question of the infinite majesty of God, "Who are you?" Three would answer. The One would say, "I am the Father." The Second would say, "I am the Son." The Third would say, "I am the Holy Spirit."

If we continued our daring question and asked, "What, then, are you?" each of the Three would answer, "I am God, the one self-subsisting, eternal, infinite Being, who knows no partner or second."

There are three Persons in one God

There lies the mystery.

Human reason at first is amazed at the statement, for it seems to go counter to a fundamental principle that when two things are equal to a third, they are equal among themselves.

Second thoughts, however, show that even in regard to the Blessed Trinity, this principle is sound and the Blessed Trinity does not contradict it. The Father *is* equal to the Son, and both Father and Son *are* indeed equal to the Holy Spirit, for all Three are God and there is no inequality in God. All Three are equal in *what* they are, that is, in their nature, but that does not prove that the Three are identical in *who* they are.

Among created things, there certainly is no parallel. Human experience never encountered a case of one numerically single nature being thrice personified or rationally individualized. But because I have not experienced a thing, I cannot argue that it is therefore impossible. Even if perchance among finite created things such multiple personification were impossible, the impossibility would be in their finiteness, their limitation, their createdness.

When we say that multiple personality of one created nature is perhaps impossible, we do not mean to imply that personality of necessity implies limitation of some sort. This is an inveterate error, which leads many people to the assertion that God cannot be personal at all, and this error is the root of all the sorts of pantheism that have afflicted the human mind. The concept of person does not in any way in itself demand limitation. It demands only self-possession, complete possession of one's nature. All we say is that, among creatures, multiple personality is perhaps impossible, for the very reason that created nature is a limited thing.

The impossibility would not lie in the essential intrinsic impossibility of multiple personality in itself. Contradictions, of course, are impossible, but there is no contradiction in saying that one numerically single infinite nature is three times personified. If a man said, "There are three Gods, and yet there is one God," he would indeed contradict himself, but no believer in the Trinity says so; he says there is one God, but three divine Persons. The nature is one; the personality is threefold.

It is a mystery indeed, but no one should wonder that God is mysterious, since God is infinite and the human mind finite. If a man would fully explain the Godhead, that man would be God, for he would have an infinite mind, since only infinite intelligence can explain an infinite thing.

There are three Persons in one God

God, then, has given a final answer to the tormenting problem of the One and the Many, but not as the ancient Gnostics, or Platonists or Averroes, or Spinoza or Hegel, who did not raise their mind beyond the totality of all mutable created things to the Creator.

To the Jew God gave the truth of the unity of God — a truth that lies indeed within the compass of human reason, but which in the course of history so few actually reached. In this truth man could rest for a while, having escaped from the confusion of the human with the divine, the confusion of the transient with the eternal, the finite with the infinite. But even after man's happy deliverance from the deepest of all errors, he was still face-to-face with the problem in its transcendent stage, and therefore he was tempted, as Spinoza the Jew and so many others, to search for a solution where it could never be found. Certainly God might have left man here on earth and perchance even hereafter without any further reply to his questioning. In His unspeakable mercy, God deigned to go further and lifted the veil a little so that we could see the ultimate solution in the light of the Godhead. It was an amazing thing that He let us see in the unity of God a Father, a Son, and a Spirit of holiness — an amazing thing, yet not a thing beyond belief.

ϫ

Human reason can ponder the mystery of the Trinity

The Blessed Trinity is a mystery in the strictest sense of the word, absolutely beyond the power of unaided human reason. It is so in regard to the fact and the nature of the fact, so that human reason could never have ascertained the fact of the three Persons in one God. Moreover, even after the fact has been revealed, it cannot strictly be proven from the principles of human reason.

On the other hand, once the Trinity has been revealed, human reason is able to do three things.

First, it can meet all objections against it. Second, it can bring comparisons, analogies, and persuasive reasonings to illustrate the mystery, and is thus able to aid the mind in its acceptance. Lastly, it can, by assuming a proposition known only by revelation, conclude to several other truths by theological deduction, and thus again facilitate its acceptance.

It is strictly of faith that human reason cannot without revelation prove the existence of the Blessed Trinity.

This is directly taught by our Lord Himself: "No one knoweth the Son but the Father; neither doth anyone know the Father but the Son and he to whom it shall please the Son to reveal Him."[2]

This truth is stressed by the anathema of the Vatican Council: "If anyone saith that there are contained in divine revelation no true and properly so-called mysteries: but that all dogmas of the faith can be understood and demonstrated from natural principles by reason, if rightly trained." In fact, from reason itself it is clear that reason could not have ascertained the fact of the Trinity. Our reason knows God only by inference from creatures. But from creatures we could never infer the Trinity in God, since in creation God is only known as Cause in the unity of His essence, not in the triplicity of His personality, for all creation is common to the three Persons.

This is not in contradiction to what is maintained in the first chapter, on the One and the Many. That chapter

[2] Matt. 11:27.

only endeavors to bring home that human reason stands before the problem of how to reconcile divine life of intelligence and will without the assumption of some duality or differentiation within the Godhead. The problem is suggested by natural reason; the actual solution can be found only by supernatural revelation.

Granted, then, that reason cannot prove the Trinity, it can show that no objections raised against it are convincing and cogent.

Suppose a man were to say: It is a fundamental principle of human thought that when two terms are identical with a third, they are identical among themselves, or, to put it in a mathematical way, if $A = B$ and $B = C$, then $A = C$. Now, the dogma is that the Father is God and the Son is God. Therefore, the Father is the Son, and there can be no distinction between them.

This difficulty can be answered thus: If two terms are identical with a third both in reality *and* in formal aspect, they are identical among themselves; I concede it. If they are identical only in reality but not in formal aspect, I do not concede it.

Let us give some illustrations. We all know that the solar spectrum — I mean the seven colors of the rainbow — *is* in reality *white light*, and each of the colors *is* that *white light,* but for all that, red is not blue, and blue is not yellow. We all know that when we have a wooden cube before us, that which is long *is* that what is broad, and that what *is* broad is the identical thing that is high, yet for all that, length is not breadth, nor is breadth height. We all know that in God His mercy *is* His justice, for divine attributes are identical with the divine essence, yet for all that, mercy is not justice.

We do not claim that these illustrations are complete comparisons with the Blessed Trinity, but we claim that they show that if A = B and B = C, both in fact and in formal aspect, only then can we say absolutely that A = C. It is quite true that the Father is God, but He is God as Father. He is the divine nature as unreceived, uncommunicated, as source communicating it to others. The Son is in fact also that same identical nature, but as received, communicated by way of intelligence, and communicating it by way of love. The Holy Spirit is that same identical nature, but received by way of love and not communicating it to any other. Hence, it does not follow that the Father is the Son, and the Father or the Son the Holy Spirit.

Now, suppose a man argued in exactly the opposite way and said: Where there are three distinct individualities or persons, there must be three distinct substances.

Therefore, since Father, Son, and Holy Spirit are distinct, they must be three Gods.

The answer is as follows: As far as our experience with created things goes, it is certainly the case that where there are three individualities or persons, there are also three distinct and separate concrete natures, but no one can show that it must of necessity be so, even in the Godhead. In created things, by multiplying individuals we also multiply natures, but the divine nature is not numerically multipliable, and you cannot show that this numerically one concrete nature cannot be held by three distinct persons. It would be impossible only if there were a self-contradiction in it, but a self-contradiction would arise only if personality were nature and nature personality, which is evidently not true.

Perchance you retort: But *you* cannot show that it is possible!

This we fully grant; we cannot show *how* it could be, nor by reason alone could we show that it is, but since God revealed it, and there is no law of thought against it, we believe it.

Suppose, again, a person makes this difficulty: What is the good of revealing a thing, which even after revelation, no one can understand? It seems an idle procedure. If I accept the Trinity, I accept only a formula, a set of words that makes gibberish to me and after which I know no more of God than I knew before.

This is perhaps the most common objection of all.

A revelation that no one could understand would indeed be an absurdity equivalent to gibberish, but when a man relates to us a fact in terms we can quite well understand, he is not talking gibberish but truth, and the human mind is made for truth.

We understand all the terms of the divine revelation. We understand what *one* means, and what *three* means. We understand what *person* and what *nature* mean. Nature is that by which a thing is the kind of thing it is. Person, in the case of rational beings, is that by which this particular rational being is this individual and not any of the others, who are as much rational beings as he, but are not he.

We understand what fatherhood is, what sonship is, and what a breathing out of holiness is. We understand what we mean by *equality*, *sameness*, *eternity*, *infinity*, *distinctness*, *relation*, *contrast*, and whatever terms we use in referring to the revealed fact. We understand the statement in which the fact is revealed quite well. The statement is so simple that a child can be made to understand it, and the statement gives us amazing information concerning the inner life of the Godhead.

What the statement does *not* do is tell us how and why these things are. Since the statement concerns the highest truth directly concerning the Godhead in Itself, this is what could be expected. A man who claimed to explain the why and the how in the Godhead would be a charlatan, and the man who believed him, an arrant fool. Only the Infinite can know the Infinite by pervading and encompassing it, and we, finite minds, have to choose between the lunatic asylum or resigning ourselves to acknowledging it.

If someone were to say that he was not interested in facts unless he could know their why and how, he would be like the man who was not interested in the life and death of his friend because no scientist has ever plumbed the mysteries of life and death.

If someone were to say that he granted that the Trinity added to his cold, abstract, metaphysical, theoretical knowledge, but that it had no practical value for his own spiritual life; that it did not make him love God or his neighbor the better; that these transcendental speculations were no real food for his soul, they were at most a difficult problem to his intellect and did not render God more lovable to him — to such a man this might be said: There is a thought that has helped many people to acquiesce in and lovingly embrace the doctrine of the Blessed Trinity.

It is this: In our idea of goodness, our idea of spiritual perfection, is included the idea of unselfishness. The good is self-diffusive. The good man wants to communicate to others what he knows and what he enjoys. Knowledge and joy seem by natural impulse to tend to pour themselves out. To know a thing and not to utter it is a strain, an embarrassment. It is hard to keep a secret, even when the truth known is sad or trifling, but it is doubly hard when the truth known is noble, happy, and glorious. Wisdom wants to spread.

It is the same with joy. Enjoyment is not complete in solitariness. If a man does not wish to share his joy with others, he is held blamable or unnatural. Complete solitary confinement is an unbearable punishment; long-protracted silence becomes a torture.

Among our fellowmen we count those best and greatest who have poured out on others the treasures of their mind and heart. The better the man, the more liberal he is with his gifts. We hold it highest praise when a man bestows his whole self on others.

Is it unlikely that in infinite goodness there is a something which in our human way of speaking we would call unselfishness, generosity, liberality, kindness, in fact the pouring out of oneself upon another? If it were so, would not the Deity become to our ideas unspeakably more lovable, more beautiful, in fact more "good"? To this question the answer suggests itself: Indeed so, but God *has* shown His goodness in the creation of this world; myriads of creatures are recipients of His bounty. All this universe is an outpouring of beauty and kindness, and we ourselves are the highest beneficiaries of the generosity of God in our gifts of mind and will, our knowledge, and our joy.

Such an answer would be true, but is it adequate? This divine outpouring of goodness is, after all, limited in time and in measure. Once upon a time, this world was not. Did, then, the object of God's bounty begin only in time and not in eternity. Did the proclamation of God's knowledge, the communication of His truth, His speech not begin before all ages?

Let us remember: this universe, however vast, is but a limited thing; it does not exhaust infinite wisdom or infinite bounty. In that sense, it is not adequate to limitless knowledge and will. It is only a creation, the work of a mighty Artificer indeed, but this Artificer did not pour

Understanding the Trinity

His whole self out in His work, since He is infinite and His work is finite. We sometimes say by way of exaggeration that a human artist puts his whole soul into his work, but this exaggeration would be foolish when applied to God, as if God could do no better. Moreover, God need never have created at all and He would still have been the infinitely "good" God.

May there not be eternally within the very Godhead itself, the complete pouring out of the infinite spiritual self on Another? The eternal divine act of unselfishness! The eternal telling of the *whole* truth to Another, the eternal sharing of eternal joy and love with Another? The eternal giving of One's whole being to Another? Intimacy of knowledge by letting Another know the whole secret of the Divinity, intimacy in enjoyment of love in the embrace of Another?

May not the Godhead be such that it contains within Its boundless reality even that which among us men we regard as the supreme moral loveliness: the giving of self, the whole of one's self, the giving to Another all one is, knows, and has? May not the Godhead be at the same time the Giver and the Recipient of infinite bounty? May not the Godhead be such that it can be given away and yet suffer no loss? Could there not be within the Godhead an infinite almsdeed not based on the distinction between poverty and riches, not creating dependence and subjection, not destroying absolute equality and yet in which One received infinite riches from the Other, in fact owed His All to Another, as a son owes it to his father, as a beloved one owes it to a lover?

I do not say that unaided human reason could have answered these questions with an undoubted affirmative, for who can plumb the infinite depths of the life of God? But after the Trinity has been revealed, the human mind bends deeper before the beauty and loveliness of God, who in the exuberance of His being knows of no selfishness, for in God Three own the Godhead, and Each owns the whole of it, since He who first in order of origin possesses it gives it to a Second, and the First and the Second give it to a Third, who, in receiving it, encompasses the full riches of the Godhead.

Those who see in the revelation of the Blessed Trinity nothing else but a stern act of God, burdening our intellect with a mystery utterly beyond us, for the sole purpose of testing our mental obedience, mistake an act of divine graciousness for an act of divine severity. Nevertheless, it remains true that this very act of graciousness requires from us our greatest act of intellectual submission, and in this sense it is our highest test of faith and our supreme act of worship.

Man is surrounded by mysteries. The more science advances, the more mysteries it encounters, the mysteries of all being, all movement, all life, the mysteries of astronomy, chemistry, biology, and whatever names man has invented for the sections of his inquiries into nature. The scientist classifies, catalogs, arranges in patterns of dependence and consequence the facts he laboriously gathers by patient investigation, but when he comes to the ultimate explanation of these myriads of facts, he is forced to acknowledge that he knows nothing. A few scientists may beguile themselves and others by inventing more intricate formulas and reciting more learned terms that the patient Greek dictionary provides, but in a moment of honesty, even they sometimes own up that they can tell you only that things are so, but why they are so, and how they are so in their innermost nature, no man can tell.

The bulk of men are strangely perverse. They find it hard and bitter to say that they do not know. In a sullen mood they will even turn to God with the utter nonsense of the saying, "I will not accept what I cannot understand." God might take them at their word and say, "Give me back, then, your life, your body, and your soul, for what do you understand of the mystery of life, of matter, or of spirit, except perchance that you are not your own handiwork but mine?"

On the other hand, a good man will stand in humility before his God and say, "Thy wisdom, O God, is greater than I can conceive and Thy knowledge beyond the uttermost bounds of my mind. Speak, and I shall believe. I shall hold true whatever Thou sayest." And God has tested the goodness and humility of man: He has revealed unto him the infinite life of the Godhead. No wonder man should stagger under the weight of that glory and should have to summon the innermost powers of his spirit supported by grace to say, "I believe."

That mighty "I believe" is, on the one hand, the deepest act of loving self-abasement before the infinite Light, as a man casts down his eyes before the blaze of the sun, not to deny it, but to acknowledge it. It is, on the other hand, the sublimest, the happiest, the proudest act of the human mind embracing truth to the utmost, now by faith, but in hope of embracing it one day by sight. It is the noblest act of worship of which man is capable, for it is the most unselfish, since it regards God for what He is in Himself. It is praise and joy that God should be what He is. It is pure adoration. It is kneeling before the throne and, forgetting oneself, singing the "Holy, holy, holy, Lord God of Saba-oth."[3] It is fulfilling one's final end and purpose as crea-ture, endowed with intelligence and will, to know Him, to love Him who deigned to make us for Himself. In this world, man is at his greatest when he bends his head and murmurs, "Glory be to the Father and to the Son and to the Holy Spirit, as it was in the beginning, is now, and ever shall be world without end." Creature though he be, he enters into the life of God. The divine Three come and make their abode in his soul in the unity of God.

[3] Cf. Isa. 6:3.

Chapter Four

✤

The Old Testament includes evidence of the Trinity

It cannot be said that the Trinity was revealed in the Old Testament, but after it has been revealed in the New, it is not difficult to find a number of indications of that mystery scattered over the pages of the Ancient Covenant. There are no texts that even remotely imply a triplicity of Persons, or a precise relation between Them, but the existence of a second Person in the Godhead is at least hinted at and seemingly implied in a number of places.

The Jews never drew the full inference from these suggestions, which now appear so plain to us. Their mind was so firmly set on the defense of the unity of the Godhead in a polytheistic world, their opposition to the multitudinous gods of the pagan pantheon was so fierce that the idea of more than one person in God would naturally be alien to their mentality, and their mind be closed to any suggestion of it. It must be recognized, however, that even had they been naturally susceptible to this suggestion, no absolutely certain or detailed conclusion could have been drawn without further divine aid and clear revelation. It is nonetheless of great interest to show the vestiges of this great mystery in pre-Messianic times, and thus follow in the footsteps of Christ.

It is well known that our Lord Himself led His hearers on to a consideration of these texts. Referring to the Messianic prophecy in Psalm 109, and having ascertained from His opponents themselves that they acknowledged the Messiah to be David's son, Christ asked, "If, then, the Messiah be David's son, how then does David in spirit call him Lord, saying: 'The Lord said unto my Lord: Sit thou on my right hand'?"[4]

Beside the psalm quoted by our Lord Himself, there are others that refer to some superhuman personage, who can be only the coming Messiah. Of this Messiah a unique Sonship is foretold: "The Lord hath said to me, 'Thou art my son; this day I have begotten thee.' "[5] "I will make him

---

[4] Cf. Matt. 22:43-44; Ps. 109:1 (RSV = Ps. 110:1).

[5] Ps. 2:7.

my firstborn, high above the kings of the earth and his throne as the days of Heaven."[6]

The most striking suggestion of a superhuman and godlike status for the Messiah is found in Daniel 7:9-14, in which the prophet saw thrones placed in Heaven and the Ancient of days, that is, the eternal God, enthroned, and then "lo, one like a Son of man came with the clouds of heaven, and He came even to the Ancient of days, and they presented Him before Him." It is most suggestive that the Messiah-Child to be born is called Emmanuel or God-with-us, that He who is to be born of a woman "is from everlasting," that among his names is El Gibbor, which means Mighty God. In the first chapter of the letter to the Hebrews, a number of texts are quoted to show that the Messiah to come exceeded in glory all the angels of God.

Independently of any passages referring to the Messiah, there is the striking personification of divine Wisdom. Anyone reading Proverbs 9 and 13, Ecclesiasticus 24:1-34,[7] Wisdom 4 and 7, and Job 10 and 15 is face-to-face with dramatic descriptions of Wisdom speaking, acting, and being

---

[6] Ps. 88:28, 30 (RSV = Ps. 89:27, 29).

[7] RSV = Sir. 24:1-34.

dealt with as a living person, in some sense the child and yet the equal of God, eternally pre-existent to this world. Those who do not accept the Trinity see in this only a literary device, but they must allow that this personification is carried to such a length that an almost irresistible impression is created of some real, subsistent, distinct personality somehow with God and in God, yet in some sense not the same in Person, although divine in nature.

The Lord possessed me in the beginning of his ways,
*   before He made anything from the beginning.*
I was set up from eternity, and of old, before the earth
*   was made.*
The depths were not as yet, and I was already
*   conceived; neither had the fountains of waters as yet*
*   sprung out.*
The mountains, with their huge bulk, had not as yet been
*   established; before the hills, I was brought forth.*
He had not yet made the earth, nor the rivers,
*   nor the poles of the world.*
When He prepared the heavens, I was present; when with
*   a certain law, and compass, He enclosed the depths;*
When He established the sky above, and poised the
*   fountains of waters;*

When He compassed the sea with its bounds, and
set a law to the waters that they should not pass
their limits;
When He balanced the foundations of the earth;
I was with him forming all things: and was delighted
every day, playing before Him at all times;
Playing in the world: and my delights were to be with
the children of men.

This famous passage from the eighth chapter of Proverbs is unfortunately weakened by the ancient Jewish translation into Greek of pre-Christian days. Instead of "The Lord possessed me," in which passage the exact Hebrew word is used, which Eve used in chapter 4 of Genesis of the conception and birth of her eldest son, the Greek reads, "The Lord *created* me." This is either a deliberate mistranslation or possibly a copyist's error. "Created me" in Greek reads *ektise me;* "possessed me," *ektesato me.* As the long *e* was pronounced *i*, the difference is slight. However, it is more likely to have been a deliberate translation, for the Greek Jews, in translating the Bible into the language of the pagans, were anxious to avoid anything that sounded too human for the spiritual transcendental God of Israel.

So likewise the passage "as a child He fostered." The Greek translated "arranging": "I was at His side arranging things." "*Harmodzousa,*" reads the Greek: "harmonizing," that is, either myself to Him, or harmonizing or arranging things in general. The Hebrew word, however, cannot mean this. The Hebrew word *amon* means a young child who is still being fostered, a child therefore who can still play as a child and amuse himself. This is evidently the metaphor or image the inspired writer had in his mind. The Jewish translators thought this probably too undignified in the context.

There exist no such vivid personifications of the third Person in the Old Testament, but "the Spirit" of God is often introduced as the immediate principle by which God creates order and gives life, light, and holiness. Such texts may be said to begin in the book of Genesis, where in the first verses we read of the Spirit of God brooding on the waters of Chaos.[8] More striking are the texts of the pouring out of gifts of holiness by the Spirit of God on the Messiah, the Servant of God, in Isaiah the prophet: "The Spirit of the Lord shall rest upon Him, the Spirit of wisdom and of understanding, counsel, fortitude, knowledge,

---

[8] Cf. Gen. 1:2.

piety and fear of the Lord." "Behold my Servant. . . . I have given my Spirit upon Him, and He shall bring forth judgment to the Gentiles." "The Spirit of the Lord is upon me because the Lord hath anointed me to preach to the meek and heal the contrite of heart."[9] Not only shall the Spirit descend on the Messiah personally, but there shall be a great outpouring of the Spirit on all flesh in Messianic days, as Ezechiel and Joel prophesy. These things were so well known that St. Peter could quote them to the crowd on Pentecost day. It is true that until that day it could not be realized that this Spirit was personal in the Godhead, but after that day, it is natural that a much deeper significance should be seen in these many texts than before.

Besides these unmistakable hints and easily recognizable indications of the mystery of the Trinity, the early Fathers of the Church often brought out others more remote, yet not without value. They emphasized that in Hebrew the word for *God* is in a plural form, *Elohim*, although the following verb is always in the singular. They pointed out that God before the creation of Adam and Eve said, "Let us make man after our image and likeness."[10]

[9] Cf. Isa. 11:2; 42:1; 61:1.
[10] Cf. Gen. 1:26.

Understanding the Trinity

They pointed to the triple "Holy, holy, holy, Lord God of Hosts,"[11] the song of praise by the angels, as implying a triplicity of Persons addressed.

They saw the Trinity foreshadowed in the apparition of the three angels who visited Abraham, of whom Abraham adored one, as Genesis 18 narrates. St. Augustine and St. Ambrose[12] have beautifully worked out the symbolism of this famous story. St. Ambrose says pointedly, "Abraham believed better than we do, although he had not yet been taught, whereas we have. No one had then as yet falsified the foreshadowing of the truth; hence, Abraham saw three persons and yet adored One."

The Fathers likewise noticed that in the Old Testament sometimes he who was styled "the angel of the Lord" is in the same context spoken of as God Himself. For instance, "the angel of the Lord" appears to Agar, yet this angel is apparently God Himself.[13] It is distinctly said both in the Hebrew and the Greek Bible that "the angel of the Lord" appeared to Moses in the burning bush, yet the Lord

[11] Isa. 6:3.

[12] St. Augustine (354-430), Bishop of Hippo; St. Ambrose (c. 340-397), Bishop of Milan.

[13] Gen. 16:7 ff.

declares that it is Himself, the God, who is.[14] A few Fathers even suggested that every vision of God in the Old Testament was in reality a manifestation of the second Person of the Trinity.

There can not be, however, a question of any real dogmatic tradition in Patristic times on the vestiges of the Trinity in the Old Testament. The majority of the Fathers certainly realized that there was no real manifestation of the Second Person as distinct from the other divine Persons before the Incarnation. They all agree that the real revelation of the mystery came through Christ our Lord, and that the Old Testament contains only faint adumbrations of this divine truth, some indeed much clearer than others, but none so plain as to unveil the truth before the coming of the Light of the world.

---

[14] Exod. 3:2, 14. The Douay-Rheims edition adds a note on 3:2: " 'The Lord appeared': That is, an angel representing God, and speaking in His name."

Chapter Five

꙾

The New Testament
reveals the Trinity more clearly

The way in which Christ revealed unto us the mystery of the Blessed Trinity is a very striking one. It was a very gradual unveiling. Briefly it might be stated thus: At His baptism in the Jordan, the heavens were opened, the Spirit of God descended upon Him in the form of a dove, and the voice of Someone was heard speaking from Heaven, saying, "This is my dearly beloved Son in whom I am well pleased."[15] Thus, three Persons come into play: one is called the Spirit and is symbolized by a dove descending; another is a Son, about to be baptized; and the third is the Speaker from above, who is evidently the Father of the One who is standing in the waters of the Jordan.

[15] Matt. 3:17.

This same triplicity of Persons had already been indicated, although somewhat more faintly, when the angel came to Mary and announced the birth of her Child. Then it was said that this Child should be called the Son of the Most High. The expression "the Most High" was a normal term for the God of Israel, the Greek word *ypsistos* rendering the Hebrew word *Elyon*. Mary asked how she would conceive, seeing that she knew not man, and in the answer of the angel, a threefold personality is suggested: the Holy Spirit is to come upon her, the power of the Most High would overshadow her, and what was to be born from her should be called "Son of God."[16] Had we not the clearer indication of the three persons at Christ's baptism, we might not have seen the implication of the text at the Annunciation, but in the light of the latter text, the former gains in significance.

Christ, then, from the beginning is somehow essentially joined as "Son" to two Others: the One, who is His Father, and the Other, who is the Spirit. During Christ's public life, He constantly refers to Himself as "the Son" and to God as His Father, and not in the way in which all creatures must call God Father in a metaphorical sense,

[16] Luke 1:32-35.

but in some special and unique way. Christ, moreover, speaks and acts so as to imply that He is not a mere creature, but possesses divinity even as the One, whom he calls Father and who is clearly the God of Heaven and earth.

This clear distinction from and yet this implied identity with the Father is a problem to His hearers. His enemies fiercely resist Christ's assertions about Himself; they want to stone Him, and they say He blasphemes because, being man, He makes Himself God. His own disciples only faintly grasp the meaning and reverently wait for further explanations. To the former He says right out, "I and the Father are one."[17] To the latter He says with a gentle rebuke: "Have I been so long a time with you and you have not known me? He that seeth me seeth the Father also."[18]

Up to the very last day of His mortal life, He leaves the revelation to this first point: the Father and He, the Son, are in some way completely distinct, and yet in another way absolutely identical, since indeed there is but one God. On the eve of His death, He finally completes the

[17] John 10:30.
[18] Cf. John 14:9.

unveiling of the mystery by promising to send another One, who proceeds from the Father and who receives from Him who is the Son. This third One is evidently God, even as the Father and the Son are God. When at last, after His Resurrection from the dead, He is about to ascend to Heaven, He proclaims that entrance into His kingdom is conditioned by reception of baptism "in the name of the Father, and of the Son, and of the Holy Spirit,"[19] thus placing all Three on a line of absolute equality, maintaining their distinctness, yet holding to the unity of God.

Ten days later, the third One comes in flaming tongues of fire and descends on the heads of those who are assembled together to form the Church, or ecclesiastical community, that Christ died to found. These disciples go out into the world, teaching and baptizing into the name of the triune God. A large section of the Jewish people most vehemently reject the new teaching and object that it is a virtual denial of the one God. The disciples of Jesus succeed in converting many Jews and many more Gentiles, and convince them that although the triplicity of persons in the unity of the Godhead is a great mystery, it does

[19] Matt. 28:19.

not militate against the absolute and unconditional acceptance of the one and indivisible God, Maker of Heaven and earth, for the Godhead remains numerically one and the same, utterly simple and unique, although it is possessed equally by the Three: Father, Son, and Holy Spirit.

Such is the briefest outline of how the doctrine of the Blessed Trinity was revealed to mankind. We can now return to the Holy Scriptures and study the matter somewhat more in detail.

It is clear that the scriptural proof of the doctrine of the Blessed Trinity is in part constituted by the proof of the true divinity of our blessed Lord. Once it is shown that our Lord, although truly man, is also true God, it of necessity follows that there are at least two persons in the Godhead. Obviously our Lord, who calls Himself "Son," is a distinct person from God the Father. If, then, both Father and Son are God, there must be more than one person in the Divinity, since there can be but one God. The proper place of the proof for our Lord's divinity is in a treatment of the Incarnation, where it is normally found.

Christ claimed Godhead and proved His claim by numberless miracles and especially by what may be called the test-miracle: His own Resurrection from the dead. If a man denies this claim, he stands before the alternative that Christ was either a knave or a fool. Either horn of this alternative is broken against the fact of Christ's life and character and the success of Christ's achievement in the Christian Church. Christianity is beyond cavil one of the greatest occurrences in the story of the human race. It must be explained, but a Christianity with a merely human Christ, who never rose from the dead, a Christ who was either fool or knave, is completely unintelligible. It has been said that it would be a greater miracle than a Christ whose claim was true and who proved it by rising from the dead.

Christ claimed Godhead not by saying crudely the bare words "I am God," but by speaking and acting continually as only God has the power and the right to speak and act. His enemies quite understood what His speech and behavior implied; therefore, they called Him a blasphemer and put Him to death. They said to Pilate, "We have a law, and according to that law He has to die, for He made Himself the Son of God."[20]

It is obvious that this claim to divine Sonship was not the normal claim of every just man to be the child of the

[20] Cf. John 19:7.

Father in Heaven in the metaphorical sense. In their eyes, it was a blasphemous claim meriting death, for it seemed to them an attack on the unity and uniqueness of God that He should have a son in the real sense of sharing with Him the divine nature.

Jewry has been and today still is one of the best witnesses that Jesus of Nazareth claimed equality with God. The recent view of some modern liberal Jews that Jesus was a good and noble man who was mistakenly credited with a claim to Godhead by ignorant and fanatical disciples belies the attitude of Jewry for almost two thousand years.

Moreover, the core and essence of historical Christianity lies in the profession of the divinity of Christ, and any thinking man would shrink from the assertion that the Christian religion, the source of untold blessings to mankind for twenty centuries, consisted in a degrading and monstrous illusion.

Here again, the suggestion of modernists that there might be a Christianity with a Christ who is not God is not only contradicted by history, but is an almost palpable failure in the present. Such Christianity is an inane speculation with no influence beyond a don's armchair and is futile outside a professor's study.

Besides such explicit statements as "I and the Father are one"[21] and "He that seeth me seeth the Father also,"[22] there are such significant sayings as "Before Abraham was made, I am";[23] "Abraham desired to see my day; he has seen it and was glad";[24] and "I saw Satan falling from Heaven,"[25] in which Christ attributes to Himself an agelong existence before His appearance on earth.

Christ claims an utterly unique relation to His Father, a relation that implies identity of nature. "All things are delivered to me by my Father, and no one knoweth the Son but the Father; neither doth anyone know the Father but the Son and he to whom it shall please the Son to reveal Him."[26] "No one can come to me [unless] the Father, who hath sent me, draw him."[27] "No one cometh to the Father but by me."[28] "I am in the Father and the Father in

---

[21] John 10:30.

[22] John 14:9.

[23] John 8:58.

[24] Cf. John 8:56.

[25] Cf. Luke 10:18.

[26] Matt. 11:27.

[27] John 6:44.

[28] Cf. John 14:6.

me."[29] "Whatsoever you shall ask the Father in my name, that will I do, that the Father may be glorified in the Son."[30] A great number of such texts can be quoted that presuppose real identity of nature between the Father and the Son, while at the same time the distinctness of the Father from the Son is clearly asserted.

In addition to this, Christ says of Himself things that exceed the bounds of creaturehood. He is "the Lord" of David, He is greater than Solomon, He is the Lord of the Sabbath. He demands belief in Himself, as He demands belief in God. He does miracles in His own name. He "wills," and the miracle is done. More than this: He gives the power to do miracles to others, and they do them in His name. He forgives sins, and He forgives much, if the sinner has loved Him. Much more than this: He gives the power of forgiving sins to others, because He has breathed on them and given them His Spirit.

All judgment is given to Him, and He will come to judge the world at the Last Day. The supreme punishment of the eternally damned is to be cursed by Him and have to go away from Him.

[29] Cf. John 10:38.
[30] John 14:13.

If anyone loves father, mother, wife, or child more than Him, he is unworthy of Him. If anyone leaves his relations for Christ's sake, Christ will give him everlasting life. It is everlasting life to know God His Father and Him. Flesh and blood cannot reveal who He is, but only His Father in Heaven can do so.

His authority is equal to that of the God of Sinai, for having quoted the Ten Commandments proclaimed on Mount Sinai, He adds to them and uses thereby the formula "You have heard that it was said of old: Thou shalt not kill, commit adultery," and so forth, but "I say unto you,"[31] with the exclusive emphasis on the pronoun *I*, since His word is equivalent to God's word, for Heaven and earth shall pass away, but His word shall not pass away. If a man wants to be perfect, then in addition to keeping the Ten Commandments, he must leave all and follow Him. When Christ leaves this earth, He claims that all authority is given to Him, and He sends His disciples to baptize all mankind in the name of His Father, and His own name, as Son, and in the name of the Holy Spirit.

This is but a briefest of some striking sayings involving a distinct claim to the possession of a divine nature

[31] Matt. 5:27.

identical with that of the Father Himself, although being distinct from Him as Son, and as man, of a lesser nature than His Father. His disciples forthwith go into the world and preach Him as the source of life and "the Prince of Glory,"[32] "the only-begotten of the Father,"[33] the Word of God, the Splendor of His Glory, the expression of His being, the Word that "in the beginning was with God," was God, and "became flesh and dwelt among men."[34]

Some scholars with a knowledge of Greek point out the fact that in the famous Prologue to the Gospel of St. John, only God the Father is styled "the God," with the Greek definite article *ho Theos*, whereas the Word is only called *theos*, "god," without that article. The passage, therefore, so they say, ought to be translated, "In the beginning was the Word and the Word was with the God, and god was the Word. He was in the beginning with the God." Upon this fact — for the wording of the Greek text no one disputes — they build a theory of the Word being only god in an "adjectival" or lesser sense. This curious error is sometimes even repeated at modernist congresses today.

[32] Cf. James 2:1.
[33] John 1:14.
[34] Cf. John 1:2, 14.

Understanding the Trinity

An impression of great learning is created by such sayings as "To me the word *god* as applied to Christ is an adjective, not a noun." What *god* as an adjective might mean no one has ever explained, unless, indeed, it means "a god" in the sense of the pagans, who had many gods. Even if the maintainers of this curious theory themselves admit a plurality of gods, is there any possible justification for imputing this weird idea to the author of the fourth Gospel? At least St. John was a monotheist and would be horrified at the thought of several gods, some adjectival, some not.

The whole theory is a mystification of a very simple thing. The use of articles in languages that possess them is ruled by custom. The Frenchman speaks of his country as *the* France, and of other countries as *the* England, *the* Germany, *the* Portugal: La France, L'Angleterre, l'Allemagne, Le Portugal; but the Frenchman does not thereby assert that there are other Frances, or Englands, Germanies, or Portugals, which are lesser kinds of Frances, Englands, Germanies, or Portugals.

The Greek Bible speaks of *ho Theos*, "the God," in rendering the Hebrew *Ha Elohim*. "In the beginning the God made the heaven and the earth . . . and the God said, 'Let there be light.' " On the other hand, in the same sentence we read, "And the Spirit of God moved upon the waters."[35] No one suggests that we should translate "the spirit of a god was moving on the waters" or that "god" there was not the Spirit of the God just mentioned before and after.

The best way to translate St. John is to take no notice of the Greek idiom, for we do not possess it in English, and to write, "In the beginning was the Word, and the Word was with God, and the Word was God. He was in the beginning with God."[36] In the sentence "the Word was God," God is indeed the predicate and describes the nature of the subject; hence, in Greek it lacks the article.

In much the same way, we in English feel the difference between "I am the king," and "I am king." In the former sentence, I assert that I am a certain well-known person designated as the king; in the latter sentence, I do not assert my identity with any person, but only my dignity, status, and power.

Now, St. John did not want to say that the Word was the identical Person just named as "the God," for the Word was another Person, but He had the same nature as the First; he was God. Since there exists only one divine

[35] Gen. 1:1-3.
[36] John 1:1.

nature, St. John had no other way to express himself than he did, and he did it with marvelous precision and brevity.

This short summary must suffice for what has been set out at length elsewhere; so vast a literature about it exists that even the most learned can scarcely know all the titles of the works concerning this central Christian truth.

If, then, we take the existence of a second Person in God as a revealed fact, the existence of a third Person remains to be proven.

The story of the Ephesian converts[37] who had never heard of the Holy Spirit is well known. Paul came to Ephesus and found certain disciples, and he said to them, " 'Have you received the Holy Spirit since ye believed?' But they said to him, 'We have not so much as heard whether there be a Holy Spirit.' And he said, 'In what then were you baptized?' Who said, 'In John's baptism.' Then Paul said, 'John baptized the people with the baptism of penance, saying that they should believe in Him who was to come after him, that is to say, in Jesus.' Having heard these things, they were baptized in the name of the Lord Jesus. And when Paul had imposed his hands on them, the Holy Spirit came upon them, and they spoke

[37] Acts 19:1-7.

with tongues and prophesied. And all the men were about twelve."

This story immediately brings to mind a previous one in many ways similar:

> When the apostles, who were in Jerusalem, had heard that Samaria had received the word of God [through the preaching of Philip, the deacon], they sent unto them Peter and John, who, when they were come, prayed for them that they might receive the Holy Spirit. For He was not as yet come upon any of them, but they were only baptized in the name of the Lord Jesus. Then they laid their hands upon them, and they received the Holy Spirit. And when Simon [Magus] saw that by the imposition of the hands of the apostles, the Holy Spirit was given, he offered them money, saying, "Give me also this power that on whomsoever I shall lay hands, he may receive the Holy Spirit."[38]

The difference between these two events lies in this: the baptism of the Samaritans was regarded as true and valid, and the baptism of the Ephesians was held as of no

[38] Acts 8:14-19.

Christian value. The Ephesians had to be properly instructed concerning the Holy Spirit. The twelve were indeed *disciples* of Jesus in some sense, they had accepted Christ and His claims, but they were amazingly ignorant concerning a vital truth of the Christian message. When they had been taught the truth about the Holy Spirit, St. Paul directed them to be baptized, and after this rite had been administered, St. Paul himself completed it by imposition of hands to bestow the Holy Spirit. We must note that in the latter passage, the Holy Spirit is referred to as *He*, that is, by the masculine pronoun as referring to a person. This is the more striking since the Greek word for *spirit* or *ghost* is of the neuter gender, and the sacred author had to do violence to grammatical rules in connecting a neuter word with a masculine pronoun. He writes, "He was not as yet come," instead of "It was not as yet come."

This conviction that the Holy Spirit was not merely a term to designate the power of God, as an attribute of the divinity, but some distinct personality, is plain from St. Peter's rebuke to Ananias: "Why hath Satan tempted thy heart that thou shouldst lie to the Holy Spirit? Thou hast not lied to men, but to God!"[39] and also to Sapphira:

[39] Acts 5:3, 4.

"Why have you agreed together to tempt the Spirit of the Lord?"[40]

St. Peter was at one with his brother Paul, who warned the leaders of the Church, "Take heed to yourselves and to the whole flock wherein the Holy Spirit hath placed you bishops to rule the church of God which He hath purchased with His own blood."[41] St. Paul remembered how, when he first began his missionary journeys, it was because the Holy Spirit had spoken to the prophets and doctors at Antioch and said, " 'Separate me Saul and Barnabas for the work whereunto I have taken them.' . . . So they being sent by the Holy Spirit went to Seleucia and from thence they sailed to Cyprus."[42] On that occasion, the Holy Spirit had spoken in the first person and commanded that these two, Paul and Barnabas, should be separated, set apart, and consecrated unto Him, and in virtue of this consecration to Him they went on their apostolic travels and exercised their ministry.

This activity of the Holy Spirit, in favor of the Christian community, St. Peter traced back to a promise of our

[40] Acts 5:9.
[41] Acts 20:28.
[42] Acts 13:2, 4.

blessed Lord. St. Peter vindicating his reception of the Gentiles into the Church, said: "When I had begun to speak, the Holy Spirit fell upon them as upon us also in the beginning. And I remembered the word of the Lord, how that He said, 'John indeed baptized with water, but you shall be baptized with the Holy Spirit.' If, then, God gave them the same grace as to us also who believed in the Lord Jesus Christ, who was I, that could withstand God?"[43] St. Peter thus traces back the doctrine of the Holy Spirit to Christ Himself, who, on Ascension day, "gave commandments by the Holy Spirit not to depart from Jerusalem, but to wait for the promise of the Father, which you have heard (saith He) by my mouth. . . . You shall receive the power of the Holy Spirit coming upon you, and you shall be witnesses to me to the uttermost part of the earth."[44] Here again the three divine Agents are placed together: the Father promises, and the Holy Spirit comes and makes the Apostles witnesses to Christ, who is the Son of the Father.

On Pentecost all were filled with the Holy Spirit and began to speak with diverse tongues, thus beginning their

[43] Acts 11:15-17.
[44] Acts 1:4, 8.

testimony as witnesses for Christ. St. Peter proclaimed that Joel's prophecy was fulfilled on that day: "I will pour out my Spirit upon all flesh," and bade all to repent and be baptized in the name of Jesus Christ for the remission of their sins. And, said Peter, "You shall receive the gift of the Holy Spirit, for the promise is to you and to your children."[45]

Our Lord then, on Ascension day, harks back to the teaching He had given them before His death upon the Cross concerning a promise of the Father to send them the Holy Spirit, and this brings us to the main passages in which our blessed Lord first reveals the existence of a third Person in God.

However, before studying this lengthy and explicit passage, we must refer to some indirect references to the Holy Spirit as a distinct personality that occur on the lips of Christ.

Matthew, Mark, and Luke tell the story of how the Jews said that Christ drove out devils by Beelzebub, the prince of devils. The Jews certainly regarded Beelzebub as an individual personal spirit who could possess the wicked and speak and act through them. They said of Christ, "He

[45] Acts 2:17, 39.

hath an unclean spirit." Christ, in answer, shows the absurdity of the Devil driving out devils, and then points out the enormity of the sin of those who made the accusation: "I say to you: every sin and blasphemy shall be forgiven men, but the blasphemy of the Spirit shall not be forgiven, and whosoever shall speak a word against the Son of Man, it shall be forgiven him, but he that shall speak against the Holy Spirit, it shall be forgiven him neither in this world nor in the world to come."[46] In this passage, the Holy Spirit is some divine Person distinct from Christ, to speak against whom is blasphemy and the unforgivable sin. Now, this Person is not God the Father, since Christ never designates His Father as His Spirit, although on very many occasions Christ refers to the Father as Him in whose name He speaks and acts and by whom He is sent. It remains, therefore, that here Christ refers to some third Person in the Divinity.

A similar hint concerning a third Person in God can be seen in Christ's words to His Apostles, warning them not to be overly anxious about what they will say when brought before the magistrates, "for the Holy Spirit will teach you in that hour what you ought to speak; it will not

[46] Matt. 12:24, 31-32.

be you who speak, but the Holy Spirit, the Spirit of your Father."[47] It is remarkable that Christ does not say, "I will suggest to you what to say or shall speak through you," nor "The Father will make you speak," but rather, "the Spirit of your Father." The real Speaker, in contrast to the human speaker, will indeed be God, but He is here designated neither as the Father nor the Son, but some third Person: the Holy Spirit, the Spirit of the Father.

We have now reached the crucial passage in which this third Person is fully revealed.

Christ is holding His last long and loving discourse with His disciples, on the eve of His Crucifixion. He has told them that He is soon to leave them and says words of comfort to them, consoling them for His departure. "I will ask the Father, and He shall give you another Paraclete that He may abide with you forever. The Spirit of truth, whom the world cannot receive, because it seeth Him not, nor knoweth Him; but you shall know Him, because He shall abide with you and shall be in you."[48]

And after a while: "These things have I spoken to you, while I abided with you, but the Paraclete, the Holy

[47] Cf. Luke 12:12; Matt. 10:20.
[48] John 14:16-17.

Spirit, whom the Father will send in my name, He will teach you all things and bring all things to your mind, whatsoever I shall have said to you."[49]

And after a while: "They hated me without cause. But when the Paraclete cometh, whom I will send you from the Father, the Spirit of truth, who proceedeth from the Father, He shall give testimony of me; and you shall give testimony, because you are with me from the beginning."[50]

And after a while: "Because I have spoken these things to you, sorrow hath filled your heart, but I tell you the truth: it is expedient to you that I go, for if I go not, the Paraclete will not come to you; but if I go, I will send Him to you. And when He is come, He will convince the world of sin and of justice and of judgment. Of sin, because they believed not in me. And of justice, because I go to the Father and you shall see me no longer. And of judgment, because the prince of this world is already judged. I have yet many things to say to you, but you cannot bear them now, but when He, the Spirit of truth, is come, He will teach you all truth. For He shall not speak of Himself; but what things soever He shall hear, He shall speak; and

[49] John 14:25-26.
[50] John 15:25-27.

the things that are to come He shall show you. He shall glorify me; because He shall receive of mine, and shall show it to you. All things soever the Father hath are mine; therefore I said that He shall receive of mine and show it to you."[51]

It is abundantly plain from these passages that Christ taught the existence within God of a third Person distinct from the Father and the Son. That this Person is within the Godhead appears from a comparison with the words that Christ uses of His own relation to the Father. It was said of Christ, "He that cometh from Heaven is above all. What He hath seen and heard, that He testifieth. . . . He that receiveth His testimony hath set to his seal: God is true! . . . The Father loveth the Son and hath given all things into His hand."[52] Christ said of Himself, "As I hear, so I judge, and my judgment is true."[53] And on another occasion, "I speak what I have seen with my Father. I have spoken the truth which I have heard of God. From God I proceeded, and came, for I came not of myself, but He sent me."[54] The

[51] John 16:6-15.
[52] John 3:31-33, 35.
[53] Cf. John 5:30.
[54] Cf. John 8:38, 40, 42.

Holy Spirit is spoken of in similar terms. He also proceeds from the Father, although He is not called Son. He is the Spirit of truth because He speaks what He hears, because He receives from the Son, who hath received all things from the Father; hence, He is another Paraclete to men, that is, another Advocate or Intercessor with the Father, even as Christ was. It was expedient to men that One should go and the Other should come. Since Christ is the Son of the Father, the other One cannot be a mere creature of the Father, for no mere created person could replace the Only-begotten of God.

What Christ had thus gradually revealed, He summed up in the final words He spoke before ascending to His Father, when He commanded all men to be baptized, that is dedicated, consecrated, surrendered, and steeped into God — as revealed in the New Covenant — that is, into the Name, the new Name of the one and only God, the Name of the Father and of the Son and of the Holy Spirit.

As Christ revealed, so taught the Apostles. The three-fold personality in the Divinity is repeatedly emphasized, and since all Christians had been baptized into the triple Name, they would easily understand. In Pauline phraseology, the term *God* is usually appropriated to the

Father, who is the source and wellspring of the Deity, and who possesses the Divinity uncommunicated, as His own and to be communicated to the *two Others*. The term *Lord,* the Old Testament word for God, which renders the Hebrew word *Jahveh,* revealed in Sinai, is usually reserved for God the Son, while *the Spirit* refers to the third Person.

So, in the form of salutation at the end of the second letter to the Corinthians: "The grace of the Lord Jesus Christ, the love of God, and the communication of the Holy Spirit be with you all." In the twelfth chapter of 1 Corinthians: "There are diversities of graces but the same Spirit; there are diversities of ministries but the same Lord; there are diversities of operations but the same God." In the fourth chapter of the letter to the Galatians: "God sent His Son, that we might receive the adoption of sons, and because you are sons, God hath sent the Spirit of His Son into your hearts crying, 'Abba, Father.' " In the fourth chapter of Ephesians: "Keep the unity of the Spirit in the bond of peace. One body and one Spirit, as you are called in one hope of your calling. One Lord, one faith, one baptism. One God and Father of all." Again, in the first chapter of 2 Corinthians: "The Son of God, Jesus Christ, was preached among you by us, for all the promises of God are in Him. Now He that confirmeth us with you in Christ, and that hath anointed us, is God, who also hath sealed us and given us the pledge of the Spirit in our hearts." In the third chapter of the epistle to Titus: "The kindness of God our Savior hath appeared. According to His mercy He saved us by the laver of regeneration and the renovation of the Holy Spirit, whom He hath poured forth upon us abundantly, through Jesus Christ, our Savior." The words *God, Christ,* and *Spirit* are as a kind of refrain running through the letters of St. Paul.

St. Peter likewise begins his first epistle with the reference to "the foreknowledge of God the Father unto the sanctification of the Spirit unto obedience and sprinkling of the blood of Jesus Christ." St. Peter tells that the Spirit of Christ manifested to the prophets of old the salvation that, by the power of God, had come upon them in those latter days and "declared to you, the Holy Spirit being sent down from Heaven." St. Peter comforts them in persecution, for they partake of the sufferings of Christ and that which is of the honor, glory, and power of God and that which is His Spirit rests upon them.

St. John the apostle similarly writes to the faithful as to those who know the truth because, says he, "you have received the unction of the Holy One and know all things . . .

and no lie is of the truth. Who is a liar but he who denieth that Jesus is the Christ? This is anti-Christ, who denieth the Father and the Son."[55] The true faithful, therefore, cannot deny the Father and the Son because they have received the unction of the Holy One.

In another place, St. John writes that the man "that overcometh the world is he that believeth that Jesus is the Son of God . . . and it is the Spirit which testifieth that Christ is the truth. We receive indeed the testimony of men, but the testimony of God is greater, for this is the testimony of God, which is greater, because he hath testified of his Son."[56]

We conclude the Scriptural testimony for the Blessed Trinity. Christ made it plain that although He was distinct from the Father, He was His true Son, possessing the same divine nature as the Father, and finally revealed a third divine Person, proceeding from the Father and sharing His nature. As Christ taught, so the Apostles preached, and their preaching was, so to say, endorsed and embodied in the very formula of admission into the Christian community.

[55] 1 John 2:20-22.
[56] 1 John 5:5, 6, 9.

Understanding the Trinity

Their baptism was in the name of the Father, and of the Son, and of the Holy Spirit, ever since the community began on the day of the coming of the Holy Spirit whom the Son had asked the Father to send on His disciples to abide with them forever.

Chapter Six

ᐠ

Tradition upholds the mystery of the Trinity

It is but natural, and to be expected from the frailty of the human mind, that a doctrine concerning the Godhead, a doctrine so profound, so mysterious, so utterly beyond human experience, should give rise to discussions, to incorrect expressions and to misunderstandings, and finally to downright error.

During the first three centuries of Christianity, no fixed technical phraseology existed to deal, so to say, scientifically and in terms of universally accepted meaning with the truths revealed in the simplest language. Moreover, the implications and the consequences of the facts revealed were not at once fully realized. It pleased God to give us the facts but to add no philosophical disquisitions about them, nor to answer the questions that the inquisitive mind of man was bound to ask concerning them and to which it was determined somehow to give a reply. The facts, in a way, were simple, and no Christian after his baptism and confirmation could possibly be ignorant of them.

There was but one and only God. The unity and unicity of God was utter and absolute, yet there were Three who were God, and the relation between these Three was expressed by Their names: Father, Son, and the One called "Breath of Holiness," for the term *Holy Spirit* really means that and nothing else. The Second and Third "proceeded," went out, from the First, the Father. These facts became more intricate by the addition of another fact: only the second One, the Son, had taken to Himself a human nature and become man and was Jesus Christ, who by His life and death had redeemed mankind. The enumeration of these facts constituted the Faith for the simple and the learned, in the beginning even as they do now.

The very word *Trinity* had not been invented. The Greek and Latin words for *being, substance, essence, person, subsistence, individual,* and *nature* had a fluid and indeterminate meaning; they lacked technical precision. One Christian writer might use them in one sense, another in another; hence, there might be real agreement with verbal disagreement, or vice versa. The Son and the

Spirit were in some sense secondary and the Father primary, for They proceeded, or came out, from Him, although they were equal to Him since they were God and God is ever the same; there can be no degrees in divinity. No wonder human speech and thought were inadequate when dealing with these divine matters, and no wonder the development of study and research in these fields would lead to incorrectness of understanding and expression, and even complete untruth unless guided by that Divine Spirit which dwells in the infallible Church that God founded.

During the first three centuries, heresies arose, which might be classed under three heads: they were either *monarchian*, or *modalist*, or *subordinationist*.

The first kind was so called in ancient days because God, especially God the Father, was held to be a sole ruler or monarch. This assertion could be based either on the denial of the divinity of Christ or on the claim that the Father Himself became man and suffered for us, but the Father, as incarnate, was called Son. Theodotus the Tanner, and his disciple Theodotus the Banker at the very end of the second century; Paul of Samosata some sixty years later; and Photinus, bishop of Sirmium in the middle of the fourth century, held this crude form of unitarianism, making of Christ a mere man. Of the second kind, styled Father-sufferers, *Patripassiani*, were Noetus of Smyrna and Praxeas, against whom Tertullian wrote.

The Modalists admitted a Trinity of Persons as far as words go, but in reality denied it. Father, Son, and Spirit were but names for the attitude of the Godhead toward created things. Originally and from eternity, God was one, but He became threefold in time. He became Creator (Father), Incarnate (Son), and the Sanctifier (Holy Spirit). The three Persons were modes or functions of really one Person, just as one individual might be priest, doctor, and magistrate. These Modalists are usually called Sabellians after their leader, Sabellius, a Libyan priest who came to Rome about 230, and after he was condemned there, returned to Egypt, where he continued to spread his errors and was vigorously combated by St. Denys the Great.[57]

The Subordinationists were those who, like Origen, were orthodox in that they held the distinction of the divine Persons and their eternal existence, yet used language that implied some inferiority, dependence, and subordination of the Son and the Holy Spirit on the Father. They

[57] St. Denys, or Dionysius (d. 268), Pope from 259.

spoke as if the Father commanded and the Son obeyed, as if the Son's divinity, in some undefined way, was less than the Father's.

The early Christian world had to face the omnipresent challenge of polytheism of their age with absolute uncompromising monotheism.

Through the doctrine of the Blessed Trinity, the difficulty was acutely felt of vindicating the unity of the Godhead in Father, Son, and Holy Spirit; the triplicity of the names could not possibly be abandoned, as they were of the essence of Christianity. In consequence, the weaker spirits, abandoning the authentic and official teaching of the Church, had sought a refuge in acknowledging either that Christ was but a man, although highly favored by God, or that the three Persons "were but three phases of one divine personality."

Finally, when, through the conversion of Constantine and the edict of toleration of A.D. 311, polytheism had become a losing cause, the spirit of polytheism made a last despairing effort to enter Christianity itself and to effect a compromise. Subordinationism is scarcely veiled polytheism, with the Son and the Spirit as subordinate or minor gods, or beings neither properly creature nor properly God.

Understanding the Trinity

The ultimate stage of this age-long warfare was by far the most momentous and the most dangerous for Christianity. The forces of error, supported by pride of place and position and even by imperial glamor, were now nominally within the precincts of Christianity, and a mortal combat was fought for the true unity and trinity of the Godhead. For a moment, the Christian world gasped in terror, for it seemed as if it had ceased to be Christian and become Arian, when all the power of the now-baptized Caesars enforced on the reluctant and sullen faithful a sham-trinity of a father with a creature-son and a creature-spirit as assistants.

The Fathers unanimously held that the Three in God were really distinct one from the other and therefore three Persons. The formulas of faith, the questions at Baptism, the testimony of pagans and heretics, and the explicit teaching of early Christian writers were all there to prove it. When heretics arose maintaining that the Three were only names for different aspects of the one divine Personality, or that the Father is God as Creator, the Son as Redeemer, and the Spirit as Sanctifier, they roused immediate opposition and were condemned. When they maintained that the Father had really suffered, since the Father and the Son are really one, they met the same opposition and were held to be heretics. So likewise, when they held the Father to be "Monarch" or sole Ruler in the Deity, and the two Others not God in the supreme and absolute sense, they were regarded as outside the pale of true Christianity.

Regarding the Son, all Fathers, while clinging to the oneness of God, taught that the origin of the Son was not by creation, that is, production out of nothing, but by procession, or coming forth, from the very substance of God the Father. They held most firmly that this procession was eternal. The Father was always the Father and always had a Son from all eternity. Never could it be said that the Son was not. These Fathers were thus essentially orthodox and had nothing in common with the heresy of the Alexandrian priest Arius, who, in the fourth century, shook the Christian world by the novel blasphemy against the Son, saying as the slogans of his error, "There was once when He was not"; "the Father produced Him out of nothing."

On the other hand, several of the Fathers were led astray into incorrect speculations and expressions by a strange fancy. The Son is the Word of God, as the Scriptures tell us. Now they distinguished between the Word *as uttered* and the Word *as dwelling within*, the Word as brought forth and the Word within the bosom of the Father. They speak as if, or at least they seem to imply, that when God created the universe, He in some sense brought forth His Word, His Wisdom, since it stands written, "The Word was God. The same was in the beginning with God. All things were made by Him and without Him was made nothing that was made."[58] To these words of St. John they joined the famous words in the eighth chapter of the book of Proverbs: "The Lord possessed me in the beginning of His ways, before He made anything from the beginning. I was set up from eternity and of old before the world was made. When He prepared the heavens, I was present. I was with Him forming all things, and was delighted every day, playing before Him at all times, playing in the world."

Misunderstanding this Old Testament metaphor of the birth of Wisdom, or at least unduly applying and stretching it, they use expressions of a generation of the Son in time, the invisible Father making Himself visible in the Son by whom He made all things. Their thought on this matter is confused, for, although saying that the Father generated His Son when He created the Universe, they presuppose and often state that this Son was with His Father before all creation and "conversed with Him,"

[58] John 1:1-3.

sunomilei, as St. Justin[59] in the second century expresses it in Greek; or he was the Father's counselor, as Theophilus[60] puts it about the same time. Tertullian[61] a little later graphically pictures how a man, before actually uttering his word has already been silently thinking and arranging within himself the word he is about to utter, speaks within his soul and allows his word to converse with him; to be his *conlocutor* is Tertullian's phrase. "So," continues Tertullian, "before the Creation, God is rightly said not to have been alone, since within Himself He had His intelligence, and in His intelligence He had the Word, whom as a second one, other to Himself, He had made by musing within Himself." One sees from this passage how early Christian thought labored to express a difficult idea, and only imperfectly succeeded.

Some modern Catholic writers hold, indeed, that the underlying thought of those early Fathers was always correct, notwithstanding faulty phrases and comparisons, but it seems better to say that *some*, at least, erred in

---

[59] St. Justin (c. 100-c. 165), philosopher and martyr.

[60] Theophilus (second century), Bishop of Antioch and apologist.

[61] Tertullian (c. 160-c225), African Church Father.

essentially connecting the existence of the Son with the creation of the universe. They are quite certain, and loudly profess, that the Son is eternal and eternally existed *in* the bosom of the Father, but they seem to imply that this is so because the Father from all eternity willed or intended to create the universe and thus from all eternity spoke this Word, His Word within Himself thus giving origin to another One within Himself. They never, of course, say outright that the Son would not have been, had the Father not from eternity thought of creating the world, but they so connect the Son with the plan of creation that there seems an essential connection between them.

Herein lies their misunderstanding. The Son arises out of the Father's intelligence by an act of self-contemplation, by the act of intelligence by which God understands His own infinite divine nature as such. This act is identical whether God is Creator or not, and creation adds nothing to the eternity, distinctness, and personality of the Son. When, therefore, very early writers say or imply that creation completed or consummated the divine generation from the Father, they are wrong in confusing manifestation with generation. The divine utterance of the Word does not mean utterance to anything outside the Deity. Within the Divinity it constitutes the Word as a distinct

Person and makes the Son distinct from the Father; it eternally constitutes both by the very opposition of the relation between the Thinker and the Thought, between the Speaker and the Word.

Admitting, then, that several early Fathers were, or may have been, incorrect in their explanation of the facts revealed, their error is totally different from the heresy of Arianism, which denied the facts themselves by stating that the Son, although existing before all other creatures, did not always exist, since He was essentially a creature. However high in dignity and God's instrument by which all things were made, Arians taught that He did not proceed from the substance of the Father, but was made out of nothing by the free will of the Father, and He was not of the same nature with God, but was only raised to some titular godhead to distinguish Him from all other creatures. This heresy overthrew the essential structure of Christianity in its central dogma, for if the Son is not God, then Christ is not God, then God did not become man and dwell among us. Arius, the man who gave his name to this fundamental heresy, was the parish priest of Baucale in Alexandria and was already advanced in age when he was condemned by his bishop, St. Alexander, for the errors concerning God the Son that he propagated.

The spread of his error was facilitated by the similarity in Greek of two words, the one *agenetos*, meaning "not becoming" or "without beginning," the other *agennetos*, "not born" or "not generated." The first is derived from *gignesthai*, "to become," "to begin to be," "to enter into existence"; the second is derived from *gennasthai*: "to be born," "to be generated." Now, it is obvious that God cannot become, begin to be, or enter into existence, for God is such that He always is, always must have existence, and has no beginning. Arius maintained that God the Father alone was really God in this sense, for the Father alone was *agennetos*, that is, unborn, and the Son lacked this essential divine attribute. The Son was born or generated from the Father; He was begotten or *genntos*. It was as if in English a man would confuse "begotten from" with "beginning from."

Juggling with the words *agenetos* and *agennetos*, which in pronunciation and sometimes in spelling were practically the same, Arius beguiled some of the clergy at Alexandria. The Son, he said, *began* from the Father, but God in the true sense, in the full real meaning, cannot "begin." Hence, the Son was not God in the sense the Father was God. True, the Son was begotten before all ages, before the time-series of this world began; true, it was a unique beginning, and the Son could not be properly classed with other creatures, for the Father did create all this universe through the Son, who stands toward this world as a god; but for all that, the Son *began* and was made out of nothing by the Father, who alone is God in the full sense.

Arius confused *origin* with *beginning*. The Son receives the divine nature from the Father, has His origin from the Father, is begotten from the Father, but derives this nature from the Father eternally, for God is always Father and always has begotten and begets His only-begotten Son.

Arius did not take his condemnation meekly. He had powerful friends, especially the sister of the Emperor Constantine, the wife of the heathen co-emperor Licinius, the persecutor of the Christians. He probably was some distant relative of hers. When deprived of his office, he wandered about the East and gained as adherent a prominent bishop, well known at court, a certain Eusebius of Nicomedia, who had been a fellow student with him under Lucian of Antioch. Arianism was from the very beginning a court-religion. Constantine the Great was certainly at first impartial; he was a statesman and a soldier and understood no theology. He professed Christianity indeed, but was baptized only shortly before his death, and by the notorious Arian Eusebius of Nicomedia. In A.D. 325 the first general council was assembled at Nicea, near Constantinople. Three hundred eighteen bishops were present, condemned Arius, and declared God the Son *homo-ousios* with God the Father.

Homo-ousios means "consubstantial." *Homo* stands for "same," and *ousia* means "substance" or "being." Constantine at first enforced its degrees, but he was gradually circumvented and finally directed the reinstatement of Arius. The son and successor of Constantine in the East, the Emperor Constantius, was a fierce and fanatical Arian, and as long as he reigned, Arianism seemed triumphant in the East. When, after the death of his two brothers, he became Emperor of the West and of all the Roman world, it seemed for a few years as if the Catholic Church was doomed and Arianism established. The thing was adroitly managed. The prominent Catholic bishops were gradually removed and driven into exile, ostensibly for other reasons, on trumpery charges in no way connected with doctrine. They were replaced by Arians. There was no Catholic bishop in Antioch for thirty years. An Arian was intruded into Alexandria. The Pope was exiled from Rome. The Bishop of Constantinople, the emperor's city, was, of course, a heretic. Constantius was succeeded in the East by Valens, likewise a fanatical Arian, although his brother, the Emperor of the West, was a Catholic. Then came for a short time the reign of Julian the Apostate. Finally God had mercy on his Church, and a Catholic emperor of East and West succeeded: Theodosius the Great.

No longer supported by the imperial court, Arianism collapsed like a pack of cards within the Roman Empire. Unfortunately, during this period of Europe, the Goths and the Vandals came into contact with the Roman Empire and adopted Christianity in the Arian form, taught by the court missionaries. The barbarian hordes that invaded North Africa, Spain, France, and Northern Italy were in their turn fierce Arians. They remained so for two centuries. The Franks were the only tribe that received the Faith directly in the Catholic form, and after them, of course, the Anglo-Saxons. The conversion of Spain to Catholicism, some ten years before St. Augustine landed in England, and the overthrow of the Ostrogoth power in Northern Italy a little later, settled the fate of barbarian Arianism; about A.D. 650 it had completely ceased to exist.

The hero of the battle against Arianism was the young deacon who accompanied his bishop, St. Alexander, at the Council of Nicea and who soon afterward succeeded him as primate of Egypt. St. Athanasius[62] saw the rise and fall of the heresy, for he was Bishop of Alexandria for forty-five years and, when almost an octogenarian, saw the reign of Theodosius the Great.

The adventures of this champion of Christendom form one of the most thrilling chapters of Church history, and even today his name is immortalized in the proverb "Athanasius against the world." He was originally driven from his see on the lying pretense of murder and immorality. He was condemned by a synod of servile bishops on the plea that he was a turbulent man and a disturber of the peace. Constantius regarded him as a personal enemy. He was five times exiled from Alexandria, but five times returned. He appealed to the Pope and was declared innocent; he went himself to Italy and the West, lying for months in hiding somewhere in Egypt, for he was the darling of his people and a great friend of the monks in the Thebaid. Several times he evaded his pursuers with hairbreadth escapes and ruses. While in hiding, he managed to send around letters and treatises in defense of the truth, for neither he nor his foes were really under the illusion

---

[62] St. Athanasius (c. 297-373), Bishop of Alexandria and Doctor.

that there was any reason for the fierce antagonism that he roused other than a purely doctrinal one; everything else was only pretense.

The Arians repeatedly drew up a number of creeds and formulas, one more craftily construed than the other, with much verbiage exalting the Son of God, but always omitting the (to them) fatal word *homo-ousios:* "of the same substance." They tried to substitute an expression that sounded similar: *homoiousios,* which means "of like substance." They were willing, at least some of them, who went by the name of Semi-Arians, to say, "of like substance in all things," but it was the precise word *homo-ousios* that they obstinately rejected, and to the defense of which St. Athanasius had devoted his life. Although he extensively used the Old and New Testaments to show the falsity of the heresy, the main stress and strength of his argument lay in his passionate cry: "We never heard of this before! It is utterly novel and strange! A Son, who is not really born, but created out of nothing! A Son who is not of the same nature as His Father! A God who was not always god, but who began in time! A Deity which comprises a real God and a lesser God!"

The Arians could not really answer this. Their tenets were novel, they had no root in tradition and antiquity, and hence, they withered away soon after state protection had been withdrawn. Their boasted irresistible logic was seen to be a flimsy sophism. To be begotten is not identical with being created or having begun; it is to receive the Godhead from One who has it in His own Person, but this reception can be from all eternity; nay, it must be, if it be Godhead at all, for nought in the Godhead is temporal. If fatherhood and sonship or generation means anything at all, it means imparting one's own nature to another, and if God the Father imparts His nature to Another, this nature is no created thing, for a god who is a creature is nonsense.

The Trinity is indeed a mystery, but it is not a foolish self-contradiction. Arianism was possible only as long as a pagan polytheistic mentality still lingered among men, when they could still imagine fanciful shadowy beings between God and this world, beings not really creatures in the same sense as we, and yet not "god" in the same sense as "God." Gibbon scoffs at the whole world being convulsed in the battle about the one letter *i*, the difference between *homo-ousios* and *homoiousios*. If Gibbon had had any historical sense, he would have seen that it was a battle between Christianity and paganism, for if the Arians had triumphed, then their Christianity would have been camouflaged polytheism, with two demi-gods styled

Son and Holy Spirit, a God who had created two other gods.

Once the true Godhead of the Son was vindicated, the battle for the Trinity was virtually won, yet the enemy still found a despairing refuge in denying the Godhead of the Holy Spirit. In the creed sanctioned at the Council of Nicea, only the short words occur: "We believe in the Holy Spirit." At the Second General Council in A.D. 381 at Constantinople, the following words were added: "Lord and Giver of life, who proceeds from the Father, who together with the Father and the Son is adored and glorified, who spake by the prophets."

By adding "the Lord and Giver of life," they formally equate the third Person with the Second. Early in the Creed, they had professed faith in "one Lord Jesus Christ," and the word *Lord,* or *Kyrios* in Greek, had been the normal divine title of God the Son. They ascribe the giving of life to the Holy Spirit, thereby signifying His equal divine power with God the Son. In the first chapter of the Gospel of St. John, it stands written of the Word of God, "In Him was life, and the life was the light of men."[63] And Christ had said of Himself, "As the Father hath life in

---

[63] John 1:4.

Himself, so He hath given to the Son also to have life in Himself";[64] "You will not come to me that you may have life";[65] "I am come that they may have life and may have it more abundantly";[66] "I know them and they follow me and I give them life everlasting";[67] "This is everlasting life: that they should know Thee, the only true God, and Jesus Christ, whom Thou hast sent."[68]

The power of giving everlasting supernatural life was essentially a divine attribute that, with the Godhead and in the Godhead, the Son had received from the Father, and as the Son, so also the Spirit, for no supernatural life in man existed except from the Father, through the Son, and in the Holy Spirit. All Christians had received the Holy Spirit and, in Him, the life of grace. The bestower of this life was the third Person, even as the Second and the First. He was not merely an instrument, a created means, but the Lifegiver Himself, for in Him the Father had poured out on all men the spirit of adoption of the sons of God.

[64] John 5:26.
[65] John 5:40.
[66] John 10:10.
[67] John 10:27-28.
[68] John 17:3.

Tradition upholds the mystery of the Trinity

After the Trinitarian heresies were condemned, the restless mind of man was for some centuries occupied with discussions and errors that directly referred to the Incarnation rather than to the doctrine of the Trinity.

In the sixth century, a certain John the Grammarian, sometimes called Philoponus, was accused of being a tritheist. He lived in Alexandria and wrote an extensive work on Aristotle. He held with Aristotle that each individual possesses his own concrete nature, and his opponents said that therefore he held three separate concrete natures in the Trinity and thus taught three gods. He strongly denied the inference.

In the eleventh century, Jean Roscelin, a Frenchman who lived for some time in England, was accounted the chief nominalist philosopher of his day. He acknowledged the concrete and the individual as the only reality corresponding to abstract concepts and ideas. His philosophical theories led him to speak of the three Persons in the Trinity as three substances — a terminology that at best is an equivocal and dangerous one.

He seems to have thought of the three Persons very much as if they were like three human souls or three angels connected only by identity of will, knowledge, and power.

Abelard assisted at his lectures and became his opponent, as was our St. Anselm of Canterbury.[69] Roscelin was Canon of Rheims and taught in several towns in France. He was condemned at Soissons in 1092 and had to revoke his trinitarian theories, but remained active until 1130.

Not long after, the Fourth Council of the Lateran in 1215 condemned a book of a famous and saintly Benedictine abbot in Italy, called Joachim de Fiore, who had written on "The Unity of the Trinity." This highly eccentric, although much venerated, man seems really to have thought of the unity of the Three Persons as only a moral and not an essential one. The reign of the Holy Spirit, he imagined, was to succeed the reign of God the Son here upon this earth. He certainly did not understand that in created things the activity of the three Persons cannot be divided or separated.

It is noteworthy that all medieval errors tended in the opposite direction to the earlier ones; they so magnified the distinction of the Persons that they were likely to be accused of believing in three gods.

[69] St. Anselm (c. 1033-1109), Archbishop of Canterbury and Doctor.

Chapter Seven

❧

God the Father
eternally begets the Son

Faith teaches us that the terms *Father* and *Son* are not merely metaphors, but describe an actual reality in God. There must, therefore, be in the Godhead a veritable and true Fatherhood and Sonship. Let us, then, strip these two ideas of all materiality and imperfection and see what their very notion essentially contains.

In earthly fatherhood in the material sphere, a father gives part of his substance in producing a son. This cannot be in the Godhead, since God is immaterial and indivisible, without any parts whatever. In earthly fatherhood, the father gives indeed to the son the same nature as he has himself, namely, manhood, but it is the same only in kind and not in number. The earthly father and his son are two completely distinct beings. They are not merely two persons, but two men constituted in the fullness of nature and person. They are two men apart from one another in the realm of existence. It cannot be so in God, for there cannot be two Gods. Hence, God the Father gives His own Godhead to the Son while remaining God Himself. The Father brings forth the Son as Person in His own image and likeness, for between the Father and the Son there is no other distinction than that of the relationship of fatherhood and sonship, origin and descent.

Stripped, then, from all imperfection, what is this divine generation? What does it have in common with human generation? It has this in common: it is the production of a living thing by another living thing from its own substance, conveying thereby its own nature to the thing produced. In God, the sameness of nature is sameness in number and therefore identity; in man, it is only in kind and therefore only similitude. We said "conveying thereby" to indicate the very purpose, aim, and direction of the act of production. In generation, the very originating act must have for aim and formal object the production of this sameness of nature, the very imparting of the nature of the Giver to the one who receives the gift.

Remember, the Father does not stand toward the Son as cause to effect. Such relationship would constitute the

Son a creature, and He is no creature, but God the Son. In creation, the Creator places the thing created out of nothing into being. The Creator exists first, and the created thing second in the order of existence. But in God, the Father does not exist first constituted in the fullness of His own being before He begets His Son.

In creation there is dependence of the effect upon the cause; there is inferiority and inequality. The created thing might not have been but for the will of its Creator. The created thing in its totality is a thing other than the Creator; it is a lesser thing in the scale and category of being. If the created thing is a spirit, it owes homage, gratitude, and obedience to its Creator, for it might never have been but for the free choice of the Creator. Its existence hangs by the thread of free will on the existence of the Creator. Had the Creator not been pleased to create, He would still have been that which He is, whereas the creature would not have been. No created thing has the reason for its existence within itself; the reason it exists lies outside itself, and any created thing lies outside its creating cause. There is no intrinsic link of necessity that binds the Creator to the creature, while, on the other hand, the creature, if it exists, owes its whole reality to Him who made it and keeps it in existence.

None of these things applies to the relation of Father and Son in the Trinity. The Son is not dependent on the Father, for it is impossible for the Son not to exist. He exists by the same divine eternal necessity as the Father; hence, He is neither unequal nor inferior. He has the reason for His being within Himself. He is not outside the Father, but is within the bosom of the Father, as the Scripture says.[70]

The Son is indeed the second Person of the Trinity, but He is not second in time, nor is He second in nature. He is not second in time, for He is eternal, and eternity knows no time. He is not second in nature, for He is God, and God's nature is of necessity numerically single and indivisible.

Father and Son, then, eternally coexist, since their very personality consists in the relationship of opposites: Origin or Source, and originated and brought forth. The Father has been called the wellspring of the Deity, but a fount is no spring without the water that rises from it. The Father is Father only because He is eternally begetting a Son. The Son is Son only because He is eternally being begotten of the Father.

[70] John 1:18.

God the Father eternally begets the Son

We might refer to the humble comparison of parallel lines. No line is parallel without the existence of another, since parallelism is protracted relation of sameness of distance. Any relation requires the coexistence of at least two terms.

The Deity, then, is such that it demands the eternal coexistence of Father and Son. The Deity is, in fact, the Father, and it is the Son, for there is no distinction between the Godhead and the Father, nor between the Godhead and the Son. The only distinction lies between the Father and the Son.

Holy Scripture, to characterize the first Person and to express His distinctness from the Son, has (with the exception of two passages) reserved the term *God* for God the Father. "This is everlasting life: that they should know Thee, the only true God, and Jesus Christ, whom Thou has sent";[71] "God so loved the world that He sent His only Son into the world."[72]

The Trinity is often expressed in the New Testament by the words *God*, *His Son*, and *His Spirit*. Our Lord, who normally referred to God by the term *Father*, also used the

[71] John 17:3.
[72] John 3:16.

sentences, "I came out from God"[73] and "I ascend unto my God";[74] and on the Cross He cried, "My God, my God!"[75]

This use of *God* for the Father has been continued in the Church and is still the normal way in the sacred Liturgy. The prayers of the Church are addressed to the "Almighty and everlasting God, through our Lord Jesus Christ, Thy Son, in the unity of the Holy Spirit, God forever and ever." This use is indicative of the fact that the Father alone possesses the Deity as His own, not received from another, not born from another, nor proceeding, but having the Godhead in virtue of His own personality, and in virtue of this personality of necessity and eternally giving it to Others.

Here the question arises as to whether the characteristic of each Person does not constitute in each case some special divine perfection, and whether in particular this fatherhood, this possessing of the Godhead of His own and the power to bestow it on another does not mean some unique perfection, one might almost say dignity for the Father. The answer must be carefully worded. The

[73] Cf. John 8:42.
[74] John 20:17.
[75] Matt. 27:46.

nature of all Three Persons is absolutely perfect and equal; in fact, it is numerically the one single divine nature, and nothing can be more perfect than God. As regards the personalities, one might answer with St. Thomas Aquinas[76] that they do not constitute "perfections" since they are mere "relatives," not "absolutes"; they are mutual attitudes of Father toward Son, Son toward Father, Spirators toward Spirit. Perfection means greater completion of being, but in a relation of one toward another, there is no increase of being.

Other theologians put it this way: formally considered, they admit, the personalities constitute perfections, even infinite perfection. Fatherhood surely, they argue, is a great perfection and dignity. But the Father has not this perfection except by having the divine Word immanent within Himself as the terminus of His infinite act of intelligence. So likewise, Father and Son have not the perfection of originating the Holy Spirit except by having the Spirit immanent within themselves as terminus of their act of will. Vice versa, the Son and the Holy Spirit have not their relative perfection except on the corresponding

[76] St. Thomas Aquinas (c. 1225-1274), Dominican philosopher, theologian, and Doctor.

condition: the Son having the Father, the Holy Spirit having Father and Son immanent within Himself. In this way, each Person in the plenitude of His perfection, and in a way corresponding to each Person — that is, in the way in which a relative has in itself the perfection of the correlative — has all the perfections of all the Persons, and thus each Person is as much as all three Persons together.

Or it might be put more simply.

Each Person is *really* identical with the divine Essence, although they are really distinct the one from the other. Hence, whatever perfection of being there is in fatherhood, in sonship, in being breathed forth, is in each, for each is the divine Essence, although each has that Essence in His own way.

There is a second name for the second Person of the Blessed Trinity. Scripture calls Him "the Word." "In the beginning was the Word, and the Word was with God, and the Word was God. . . . And the Word became flesh, and dwelt among us."[77]

Now, *word* means utterance of thought. This utterance need not be by sound or syllable; one can *think* a word. By

---

[77] John 1:1, 14.

word we need not mean some compound of letters formed by lips in some language; we need not make it physical, but can leave it purely mental. When a thinker realizes his own thought, his concept, his idea, when he acknowledges it as such to himself and, so to say, places it over against himself as the fruit and outcome of his own act, his thought becomes his "word" to him. Maybe his lips do not move, maybe in his brain there is no imaginary echo of any part of human speech, yet it is his utterance to himself as mind, as thinking subject. The Greeks would say it is his *Logos,* for which there is in English no better rendering than "word." Unfortunately, in English the term *word* is apt to recall sounds of vowels and consonants. We must strip it of all association with acoustics and realize it as the mental double, the thought-replica of the thinker, the object of his understanding in contrast to himself as subject.

God deigned to use this term *word* of His only-begotten Son, so that we might thereby better grasp the mysterious truth about that divine Son.

By the light of this new revealed name for the second Person, we are enabled to gaze a little deeper into the meaning of the mystery.

God is a spirit, and since we, too, are spirits, we are able, by the study of ourselves, to progress a little in the understanding of God. We men possess the curious power of mentally doubling up against ourselves. We often gaze at ourselves; we read or guess our own motives. We are given to self-study. We praise or blame ourselves. In a measure we understand ourselves, and we know that we know.

Sometimes the picture, or rather the idea of what we are, stands vividly opposite our own mind. We look at it, we recognize it, we may admire it or loathe it, but there it is, unmistakable, and we say complacently or reluctantly, "That is I." We have uttered ourselves to ourselves.

It is a mysterious thing, this spiritual power of being at the same time subject and object, at the same time the thinker and the thought, this understanding of self, this production of self in a way outside oneself. Mark that I said "in a way"; it is not completely correct to say that I have placed myself outside myself, since I always remain the one single person I am. I am a limited, created, finite being. I cannot really go beyond the boundaries of my own circumscribed individuality. I cannot really duplicate my personality, for it is linked to the finiteness of my created nature. It is only a self-modification, a self-change that I can achieve. I can place myself in two opposite positions or attitudes at once, since, as spirit, I am at least not hampered by the restraints of matter; thus I can be on-looker of my own actions and thinker of myself, and utter to myself my own name.

This truth God has deigned to use to give me some conception of the birth of His Son. He said to us, "My Son is my Word. In stark reality He is other than I, for I am the Father, and He is my Son. He is my Son, because I think Him. I beget Him by my act of infinite self-knowledge; I utter Him as the infinite object of my thought. I am a living God, and my life is thought. Being God, I know my Godhead, and what I know is my Son. I am the source of the Godhead, and He is the Godhead as uttered by Infinite Intelligence. He is not I, although He and I are the same one God."

There lies the mystery of the divine life of the eternal Spirit. The divine Mind is a twofold subsistence or person: that of the Sayer and that of the Word said — eternally distinct, yet eternally together; in absolute equality, yet in infinite otherness!

God has deigned to give us yet a third expression concerning His Son, which can aid us in our thoughts concerning the eternal birth from the Father.

We read of "His Son, whom He hath appointed Heir of all things, by whom also He made the world, who [is] the brightness of His glory and the figure of His substance, up-holding all things by His power."[78]

Here we must specially study the crucial words "the brightness of His glory and the figure of His substance." The Greek runs the *apaugasma* of his glory, and the *charakter* of his hypostasis. *Apaugasma* means strictly "the efflux of light," "effulgence," "radiance." *Ayge* is the Greek word for "sunlight," the highest intensity of light possible, and *apaugasma* is what is sent forth by this light; hence, its splendor and dazzle, the beams of its brilliance.

The sacred author clearly uses a metaphor taken from the realm of light. God is like the blazing disk of the sun at noonday, and God's only-begotten One is the brightness of its light. Thus, the Son shows forth the Father and is His utterance even as the Word is His utterance in the realm of thought. He goes forth from the Father, yet He does not leave the Father, even as the splendor of light shines forth and yet is not severed from the light itself, its source and origin.

The Greek words "character of His hypostasis" are rather clumsily rendered by "figure of His substance." It would be better to translate them as "the express image, the exact

[78] Heb. 1:2-3.

expression, of His subsistence"; that is, the Person of God the Father. *Character* in Greek originally referred to the engraving upon a seal and then to the image on the wax, which is the direct replica of that upon the metal, and thus its precise expression. Even the inspired author, when speaking of God, must use human terms taken from simple things, and here he uses the simile of the die that, by being stamped, reproduces itself. The Son, then, is the utter image and counterpart of the Father.

This thought is in St. Paul's mind also when he speaks of "the Son of His love, who is the image of the invisible God, born before all creatures"[79] and of "the glory of Christ, who is the image of God."[80]

A man, by looking into a mirror, sees his own likeness. God, eternally looking at Himself, not only sees, but produces, His own image, and the living image of Himself is His only-begotten Son. Thus, divine gaze meets divine gaze, and of that act of infinite understanding it is written, "No one knows the Son but the Father, and no one knows the Father but the Son."[81]

---

[79] Cf. Col. 1:13, 15.

[80] 2 Cor. 4:4.

[81] Matt. 11:27.

We creatures, when we hear of fatherhood in God, must necessarily begin our investigation with a study of human fatherhood on earth. This human fatherhood is so great, so well known a fact in human affairs, that it seems to us the most solid fact, the most substantial reality we can think of. Moreover, fatherhood and parentage seem the dominating feature in all living nature, whether of beasts or plants, although in nonrational nature it is but the physical fact of descent without recognition, without mental understanding of fatherhood.

This may lead us to regard earthly fatherhood as the real thing and divine fatherhood as the attenuated shadow of the great reality, since we have to think away so many conditions and circumstances of human fatherhood before we arrive at the fatherhood of God. But we Christians know that it is not so; "for this cause we bow our knees to the Father of our Lord Jesus Christ, of whom all paternity in Heaven and earth is named."[82] It is God's fatherhood that is first in eternal and infinite perfection; created paternity here below is but a lightsome shadow, a faint outline and replica of the everlasting great reality above. In the human title of "father," there is but a created

[82] Eph. 3:14-15.

114

similitude of the might and majesty, the dignity and awesome grandeur, the tenderness and understanding that lies in the divine name *Father* as known by the only-begotten Son of God.

A ray of the glory of that Fatherhood has traveled the infinite distance between God and man and shone on this our world here below. In the prism of our materiality, this ray has been broken and divided so that it might be shared by men and women each in a distinct way, thus displaying the riches of the parenthood of God.

People have curiously asked why God reserved this glory for mankind since He did not give it to His angels, however resplendent they may be in their nine choirs before His throne. The angels are spirits, even as God is spirit, yet none of the angels exists the one *because of* the other; none dare call the other "my son."

Angelic minds, however vast, yet are created and limited. They are indeed light, but borrowed light, and they cannot give that light away and enkindle another light like unto themselves. Were they capable of division, and were their nature somehow made up of parts, perchance it might have been done, but since they are indivisible intelligences, they could only give the totality of their being away, while remaining as they were, even as the Father gives the Godhead to the Son. This for them is impossible. They cannot give themselves away, since they are not utterly their own; they are God's who created them. They cannot give themselves away, for their nature is limited, and limited equalities withdrawn from limited equalities leave no residue.

God the Father is infinite, and infinitude can suffer no diminution even when possessed by another. God the Father has the divinity in infinite right, and His possession thereof is of infinite completeness. Hence, He still possesses it when Another owns it even as He.

When, however, God created man, and in creating man wedded matter to spirit, from this wedding of soul and body the possibility of human parenthood arose, and God deigned to create here on earth some similitude of His triune glory in the human family of father, mother, and child. And now we men can use this reality so well known among ourselves to understand a little of what goes on within the Godhead.

God revealed the Blessed Trinity to the angels, and to them He may have made use of other modes of unveiling the truth than to us, but we shall always best understand the statement of the divine mystery in the words "God is a Father, who has a Son."

God the Father eternally begets the Son

Ever since God revealed the Trinity, the sea of divine glory is to us no undifferentiated dead whiteness, well-nigh blinding our eyes and dazing our mind, showing us nothing but eternal, unchangeable infinite sameness, as if it were activity without principle, aim or achievement within itself, ceaseless energy without production, without the joy of completion. For us God has ceased to be the Great Unknown, of which we knew only that He made this world, the free sport of divine artistry, betraying yet hiding by infinite remoteness the Artist who made it. We still, like Moses, put off the sandals of our feet when in the desert of dry philosophy we approach the burning bush and hear God Himself saying, "I am who am."[83] In adoring gratitude we thank Him still for His gracious speech to Israel of old, but we are glad that in the fullness of time He told us more, and told us, "I am Father, and I am Son, and I am Holy Spirit."

If we let our reason dwell for a while on the amazing truth thus laid open to our minds, it is natural that we should start asking ourselves questions. First, what precisely is it that constitutes each Person in His own personality? We are not asking in general what makes each

[83] Exod. 3:14.

117

Person a person, for the answer to that is obvious: since a person is a self-subsisting individual of an intellectual nature, divine Persons, even as human or angelic persons, are constituted by being distinct subsistencies of an intellectual nature. We are asking not why is the Father a person, or the Son and the Holy Spirit persons, but why is the Father father, the Son son, the Holy Spirit Holy Spirit? What constitutes each in His personality?

We realize that it would certainly be wrong to think that each Person had some absolute divine quality, property, or characteristic that the two Others did not possess and by which He differed from the Others, thereby becoming distinct from them. Such an idea would introduce grades of perfection between the Persons; it would introduce some real composition in the Godhead, as if it were made up of a variety of perfections. Such an idea is clearly wrong.

Can we conclude that it would be right to say, as St. Bonaventure[84] does, apparently copying St. John Damascene,[85] that the Persons are constituted by their origins,

---

[84] St. Bonaventure (1221-1274), Franciscan mystical theologian and scholastic, writer, bishop, and Doctor.

[85] St. John Damascene (c. 676-749), theologian, writer, scholar, and Father and Doctor of the Church.

so that the first Person is formally constituted by His act of generation, the Son by His passive generation — that is, by being generated — and the Holy Spirit by His being breathed out? Yes, it would be right, but it would be perhaps better to express the same underlying thought in a somewhat different way, as St. Thomas Aquinas does: that each Person is constituted by His relation to the Other in origin. Each Person is the divine Essence formally as a relation within the Godhead. This relation is one of origin, as we know, and if viewed as act, it is indeed origin, but if viewed as constitutive principle, it is a relation, the relation between the Originator and the Originated.

One might here perhaps suggest that this creates a seeming contradiction when applied to God the Father, since His relation toward the Son being that of Generator toward Generated, or First Origin toward the Originated, He, the Father, at least, must be constituted in Personality before and independently of the act of generation. But this is only a seeming contradiction. The Father is not first a Person constituted in personality in some vague and general way in order to generate and then be Father, but He is constituted in personality precisely by being Father. He is both Person and Father by the very act, necessary, eternal, and relative of generation.

Understanding the Trinity

Or we can perhaps put it still more plainly: this necessary, eternal divine act, I mean the divine substantial understanding, which by the necessity of its nature eternally produces and possesses the immanent Word as produced — that *is* the Father. We should not think of the divine generation first and then of divine fatherhood as a kind of consequence, for the Father, under the formal aspect as father, is *this* person and generates, and through this very act of generation eternal, necessary, and relative, is a distinct person — namely, the Father. We should altogether banish from our thoughts or our imagination some sort of indeterminate person who becomes the Father only in consequence of His generation, but who would still be a person on the, of course, impossible supposition that He did not generate.

Let us halt for a moment and consider two very difficult points, which have reference to both the relation of Father to Son and that of Father and Son to the Holy Spirit, lest a misunderstanding should arise that would completely vitiate our grasp of the mystery. We have explained that the Son has been born and is being born of the Father, has been uttered, and is being uttered by Him as His Word, that He has shone forth, and is now shining forth as the Light from the eternal Light. Such expressions might easily lead us to regard the Blessed Trinity as a sort of work or process, labor and operation, which was begun before all ages and now is still going on. But the infinite act of generation in the Godhead is not a work in never-ending progress.

All labor among men is of necessity a tending toward achievement, but when the achievement has been reached and the object of the activity exists, the labor then ceases. Moreover, in created things, all activity is a transition from the state of mere potency or power to the state of actuality.

None of this applies to the Blessed Trinity. We may indeed say that God the Son is being born from the Father, lest we should think of divine generation as a thing of the past, as if by an act, now over and gone, the Father once generated the Son, who now, in consequence, exists independently of the Father.

We should, however, always remember that the Son is always constituted Son in the fullness of sonship and not at long last as the end of a process of labor. This is so, not only because in God there is no time and therefore no before and after, but also because the generation of the Son and likewise the production of the Holy Spirit is not an operation in our human fashion, but simply an infinite fact. It is quite true that God is pure act, for there is in God no unrealized potency waiting for fulfillment.

While God is what to us is incessant activity, He is also the fully existent complete reality, and the Trinity is not something that *becomes;* the Trinity eternally *is.* It is the Three who stand — the First and Second stand toward one another as Father to Son, and the Third stands toward the Others as One breathed forth by the breath of Two, who breathe Him out in Holiness.

The three divine Persons, while one substance, essence, and being, are three subsistent relatives by the relation of being opposites. Their whole personality consists in their relation to one another. In other words, the whole personality of the Father consists in His very Fatherhood, that of the Son in His Sonship, that of the Spirit in being spirated or breathed out by the other Two.

As persons They are eternal opposites, but in nature and substance They are one "thing": the Godhead. The Father and the Son together are not more than the Father alone, or the Son alone, nor are all Three more than the Two. Relativeness does not add to being or substance, precisely because it is pure relativeness. The relation of being parallel of two lines does not add to their length or thickness. It all comes again to this: there are three Persons, not three natures, and the Persons are constituted by their "opposition" or contrast one to the other.

There remains the second difficult point, which is this: the Son is generated by the intellect of the Father, the Holy Spirit by the will of Father and Son. But intellect and will are involved in the divine nature, and hence must be common to all three Persons, since They all possess the same identical intellectual volitional nature. In what sense, then, is the Son the thought of the Father and the Spirit the love of Father and Son?

We reply as follows: the Father produces the Son by that very intellect which is common to all Three, but He does so inasmuch as He has this intellect in and from Himself and not by generation, not by any communication or bestowal from someone else. In Him it is originated and unbegotten and unproduced, and it is the Father alone who thus produces by the intellect, and not the Son, nor the Holy Spirit. Since the Father possesses this intellect from and of Himself before all production, He can communicate it to another Person. The Son and the Spirit have it imparted from the first Person and do not impart it to any further Person because in Them the intellect has already its own infinite and adequate object and act that cannot be multiplied.

Understanding the Trinity

Should it perhaps be objected that if one Person generates by the intellect, the other Two must do so also, the reply is at hand: not all Persons have intellect of themselves; the second and third Persons have intellect communicated to them from Another. In order to generate, it is not sufficient to have the divine intellect, but it must be possessed of oneself and not received. Of the three Persons, only He who has the divine intelligence of himself generates, since He is prior in order of origin to Him to whom He communicates it. The principle of the divine generation is therefore not divine intelligence considered in the absolute, but divine intelligence as possessed by the Father as eternally His own.

The same we must say of the act of love that produces the Holy Spirit. Divine love is of the essence of the divine nature, and therefore common to all three Persons, but only the Father and the Son possess it of themselves, as their own, unreceived; therefore they communicate it to the Third, who does not communicate it any further because in Him divine love has its adequate infinite fulfillment as person.

It is true that the Son, like the Holy Spirit, has received the divine nature from the Father, and therefore has therein received the act of infinite love. But the Son received it by way of intellect and not by way of will or by way of love; hence, until the divine nature is handed on to Another by way of will and the Two who possess it breathe out Their love, the Trinity has not received its completeness.

༄

Chapter Eight

The Holy Spirit proceeds from the Father and the Son

The third Person of the Trinity is to us the most mysterious one of all Three. Let us see, however, what adoring contemplation and reverent study can gather from what has been revealed.

First, there is the name itself. He is called the Holy Spirit. By *spirit* in general we usually mean an incorporeal and intelligent being. A spirit has no body. It exists, but is totally immaterial; it has no length, breadth, size, shape, or weight, and thus belongs to another class of beings than those we can reach by our five senses. But a spirit thinks and wills; in other words, it is a free intelligent unit, the center of its own actions and responsibilities.

Our souls are spiritual inasmuch as we think and will and are free. Our souls during our stay on earth are also the life principle of our body, and even after death crave for reunion with matter that they may perform *all* their functions, not only thinking and willing. Our souls are therefore not pure spirits, yet because they are existing units exercising spiritual activities, we have a clear idea what spirits are; they are just like ourselves and act as we do with the exception of our corporeal material activities.

God is a Spirit. We thereby mean that God is a Being who is intelligent; that is, He thinks and wills and is free, but has no body.

All this is, of course, true of the Holy Spirit, but do we mean just this when we call Him Spirit?

No, for this applies equally to God the Father and God the Son, and we are now dealing with the distinctive name of the third Person by which He is differentiated from the first Two.

What, then, do we mean? We mean *Spirit* in its aboriginal and first meaning, namely, Breath. *Spirare* in Latin means "to breathe." The Greek word is *pneuma*, from *pneo*, "to breathe." In Semitic (Hebrew, Aramaic) the word is *ruha*, likewise from *riah*, "to breathe." (Ghost, from Saxon *gast*, "breath.")

The second Person is a Son; hence, he is *born*. The third Person is a Spirit; hence, He is *breathed forth*. On Easter evening, our Lord came to His disciples and "breathed on them and said, 'Receive the Holy Spirit; whose sins you shall forgive, they are forgiven them.' "[86] Our Lord said that the Paraclete "comes forth" (proceeds) from the Father. It is noticeable that although our Lord repeatedly said, "I came forth from the Father," He never used in His own case the same word He used in the case of the Holy Spirit, the Greek word *ekporeuesthai*, which is well rendered by the English "proceed," which suggests a formal, deliberate, self-conscious, almost ceremonial "procession-like" walking out or carrying oneself forward. The Greek verb possessed an active form that directly means "to carry away or forth." We still say in English that a man carries himself well or has a good carriage when he moves forward in dignified and stately fashion. Moreover, the Greek verb can be taken in a passive as well as a medial form, and mean "to be brought forth."

The special terminology may well be due to our Lord's wish to indicate that the Holy Spirit comes forth from the Father in some other way than He does from the Father by birth. It is striking that the term *ekporeuesthai* is used eight times in the New Testament for what proceeds from the

[86] John 20:22-23.

mouth (whether of God or man), which shows how close the term is to being "breathed out." In human life, the verb *breathing out* is, apart from its corporeal meaning, used of vehement acts of the will: a man breathes love or hatred, threats and violence, kindness and benevolence, affection and goodwill, or detestation and loathing.

This meaning must be an analogy to the meaning when applied to the Godhead. It must have some connection with the divine will rather than the divine intellect. The intellect does not breathe out its ideas; it conceives them and gives them birth. It is the will that breathes out love; the will has its aspirations. A man aspires to a thing when he wills it.

Now, the third Person is a spirit of holiness. Since all three Persons are equally holy, why should the Third be a spirit of holiness? What is holiness? Rectitude of will. A man is a good man when he wills all that is good for himself, for his neighbor, and, above all, that which is in conformity with the supreme Good, who is God.

We are good if we, during our trial on earth, want God and seek God. After death we are holy because we shall be eternally joined to God in delight and joy.

Holiness in God is the will and enjoyment of His own infinite goodness. It is the love of His own infinite being.

Now, love seems to demand some duality of lover and beloved. Our human reason might have faintly surmised that perhaps this might be true even of the Godhead, but we could never have known the fact. But God has deigned to reveal that it is indeed so, and that it is so in a way beyond our understanding.

God as holiness, that is, as love or will, is a distinct Person breathed out by the Father and the Son. We human beings, when speaking of such ineffable things, must use analogies and metaphors. We, as it were, picture to ourselves how out of the embrace of the Father and the Son, that is, the infinite Knower and the infinitely Known, there leaps forth the Third: the infinite Beloved; and each of the Three is the same one God, with all the fullness of divine intelligence and will. Thus, we have the infinite, eternal life of the Three-in-One Being, Knowledge, and Joy. The Three being distinct with an infinite eternal distinctness that constitutes them three Persons and yet all Three being the one divine single substance, their distinctness being their mutual relation of opposite or contrast: God, His Word, and their Love; Father, Son, and Holy Spirit.

It would be wrong to say that the Three share the Godhead. A share means a division, a distribution in parts.

The Godhead cannot be divided; it has no parts. We do not speak of sharing when each has and is the whole. The Father is all that the Son is, but He is not who the Son is, nor is the Son who the Father is. The Spirit is all that Father and Son are, and either of Them is; but He is not who the Father nor who the Son is. He consists in His personality precisely by His infinite contrast to Them.

It is remarkable that the Holy Spirit in Scripture is so emphatically called the Spirit of Truth. One would at first have expected that the Son, being the wisdom of the Father and His uttered Word, should be characterized by the name of Truth rather than the third Person, who is holiness and love.

The spontaneous answer to this difficulty would be that spirit of Truth means in Christ's promise the Spirit who imparts the truth to the minds of men. This seems plain from the very context of Christ's words: "The Paraclete, the Holy Spirit, will teach you all things"; "When He, the Spirit of Truth is come, He will teach you all truth."[87]

This answer is true, but not complete. Imparting truth to created minds of angels and men is a work of God *outward*, as the technical term runs, and therefore belongs to

[87] Cf. John 14:26; 16:13.

the three Persons equally. If the imparting of truth is ascribed to the third Person, it is because such appropriation is a help to us to understand the character of the Person in Himself.

Let us note, then, that the third Person is called not the Truth, but the Spirit of Truth.

Now, what is truth? It is the equation of thing and thought, the relation of mind and object, of intelligence and reality. The self-understanding of the infinite Reality which is God, that is, the highest truth, and the two terms of that equation are God and His Word, the Father and His Son. "No one knoweth the Son but the Father, and no one knoweth the Father but the Son.[88]

The Holy Spirit, then, is aptly called the Spirit of Truth, for He is the Spirit of the Father and the Son. Our Lord mysteriously indicates this character of the Holy Spirit as the Breath of Truth by saying, "He shall not speak of Himself, but what things soever He shall hear, He shall speak";[89] "He shall glorify me because He shall receive of mine and show it to you. All things whatsoever the Father hath are mine. Therefore I said that He shall receive of

[88] Matt. 11:27.
[89] John 16:13.

mine and show it to you."[90] When, therefore, truth concerning God is imparted to men, it is right that this should be called the coming of the Holy Spirit, since it is the Truth breathed out in grace and love which is given to men.

It must be well remembered that in the Blessed Trinity it is not the divine nature formally as such that produces the three divine Persons, as if all Three arose and took their origin from the divine nature considered in itself. This would be a complete misunderstanding and against authoritative teaching. The Son proceeds from the Father *as* person, and the Holy Spirit proceeds from Father and Son *as* persons, whereas the Father does not proceed at all. The Father has no origin of any kind. His personality is such that He possesses the divinity as His own and gives it to the Others. He is Himself the source and wellspring of the Godhead, as the Greek Fathers truly express it.

We see, therefore, how aptly the Scriptures normally reserve the word *God* to God the Father, when they speak of God and His Son and His Spirit. At first this practical limitation of the use of the term *God* to the Father might seem strange, and it has led heretics, old and new, to a triumphant erroneous conclusion that the Father alone is

[90] John 16:14-15.

God in the real sense of the word, the other two Persons in a secondary sense only.

The conclusion is a subtle perversion of truth. It is quite true that the Son is God in a secondary sense, in that He is indeed the second Person of the Trinity. It is quite true that the Holy Spirit is God in a tertiary sense, for He is indeed the third Person of the Trinity. It is quite true that the Father is God in a primary sense, for He is the first Person of the Trinity. The subtle error creeps in when this priority of order is changed into a priority of time, for there is no time in the Godhead.

The error is deepened when this priority of order is changed into a priority of inequality, a priority between dependence and independence. The Father is as "dependent" on the Son as the Son is on the Father, for Father and Son are eternal correlatives.

The error becomes deeper still when this priority is construed as one of nature rather than of person, as if the divine nature could exist in a greater or a lesser degree, and as if, therefore, the Son or the Holy Spirit was a little less divine than the Father. One might as well say that of two parallel lines one was a little less parallel than the other. It is the Godhead itself that the person of the Father eternally gives to the Son, and the Son together with the Father gives to the Holy Spirit, and in the Godhead all is infinite, eternal, sovereign, and independent.

If the Trinity is explained as a kind of gradation of the divine nature, then the mystery is perverted into a self-contradiction, a metaphysical impossibility, which the human mind must of necessity repudiate, and which no man can believe if he understands what he says, for gradations of divinity are mere and utter nonsense. The divinity is the absolute, and the absolute has no degrees. A graded absolute is a square circle.

Granted, then, all this and all this well understood, there is nothing strange in the fact that Holy Writ normally limits the use of the word *God* to the Father and speaks of God, His Son, and His Spirit, since God the Father gives the Godhead to the Others and thus is the source and wellspring out of which the two Others eternally arise. Holy Writ, by its normal usage of the term *God* of God the Father, thereby helps us to understand the special characteristic by which the Father is distinct from the Son; that is, that the Father has the divinity uncommunicated from any.

Because of the mysteriousness of the third Person to our understanding, God has deigned to express by many symbols and emblems the character of the Holy Spirit as

Person: a hovering dove, a flame overhead, a rushing wind, a lightsome cloud, a thing received, a gift, a dweller in a temple, another Paraclete, One who prays within us, a fire in which one is merged or baptized.

According to the Gospels, at the baptism of Christ, the Holy Spirit descended from Heaven in a bodily shape as if it were a dove and remained or rested upon our Lord.[91]

The symbol of the dove was doubtless meant to recall to our mind the account in Genesis: "Darkness was upon the face of the deep, and the Spirit of God brooded over the waters, and God said, 'Let there be light, and there was light.'"[92] In Genesis, the Spirit of God is pictured as brooding like a bird over chaos and darkness, and thus fecundating it through Its fostering care and pervading power. At Christ's baptism, the unity of the three Persons was made clear by the three divine Agents: the Father speaking, the Son standing in the waters submitting to baptism, and the Holy Spirit descending from on high. The appearance of the dove must have signified that the Incarnation, viewed as the supreme sanctification of a human nature through assumption into personal union with

[91] Matt. 3:16; Mark 1:10; Luke 3:22; John 1:32.
[92] Gen. 1:2-3.

the Son, was to be ascribed and appropriated to the Holy Spirit. Thus endorsing the word of God's ambassador to the Virgin-Mother: "Thou shalt conceive and bring forth a Son. . . . The Holy Spirit shall come upon thee, and the power of the Most High shall overshadow thee, and therefore also the Holy One which shall be born of thee shall be called the Son of God."[93]

Christ's baptism is an attestation that what had been foretold had been accomplished. This appropriation of the work of the Incarnation to the Holy Spirit is forever embodied in the Apostles' Creed: "Conceived through the Holy Spirit, born of the Virgin Mary"; and in the Nicene Creed: "Incarnate through the Holy Spirit, born of the Virgin, He became man."

It is obvious that all three Persons sanctified the human nature of our Lord as something created, although only one Person assumed it as His own. This sanctification, however, is ascribed to the third Person as the subsistent holiness of God, thereby revealing to us His special characteristic as Person. For this characteristic, the brooding dove was a fit emblem. Should it be asked why not another bird was chosen for this symbol — say,

[93] Luke 1:31, 35.

an eagle or a falcon — it is easy to give the reason: that God on this occasion wished for no emblem of might or swiftness, but an emblem of that still and tender power of imparting life, which man's imagination joins to the nature of the dove, with which man also associates that of innocence, or sinlessness, which was specially fitting at the baptism of Christ.

In the Christian mind and usage, the name *Paraclete* or *Comforter* is undoubtedly a distinctive name for the Holy Spirit, and rightly so. We should, however, always remember that He is called by our Lord "*another* Paraclete," promised after the departure of our Lord, who is thus by implication called the first Paraclete.

What our Lord meant in this parting discourse to His disciples is this: "Until now, through my bodily presence, through my audible words and visible miracles, through the attraction and lovableness of my human nature, I have been your comforter in all your difficulties. All this is going to be withdrawn after my Ascension, when you will see me no longer. But all this will be replaced by the coming of the Holy Spirit, that is, by the direct work of divine grace in your hearts. In this sense, I as God — incarnate, visibly dwelling among you — shall no longer be your comforter, but the Giver of all grace, the Father on high, will send you Him who is the supremely comforting Gift to every human heart."

"Because I said that I go, sorrow hath filled your heart," said our Lord. "But another source of inner joy shall be given you — the presence of Him who is the subsistent joy of God: the Holy Spirit."

Our Lord laid special stress on the work of this new Paraclete as that of teaching and giving truth, because in the minds of the Apostles, the absence of a Teacher was felt as the greatest hardship, since they realized how little as yet they understood and remembered of what Jesus, their Teacher, had told them. The new Teacher would re-call to their mind all that their first Teacher had told them, and even tell them many things that the first Teacher had not told them, for they could not understand them as yet. The English hymn, therefore, should run:

> *Thou who art called a Paraclete,*
> *Best Gift of God above,*
> *The living Spring, the living Fire,*
> *Sweet unction and true love.*

If we say *the* Paraclete, it must be understood that He is *the* Comforter in our present state, since the Ascension of our blessed Lord.

The Holy Spirit is often called *the Gift*. In the Greek Catholic Church, Confirmation is bestowed during the anointing by the simple words "The Gift of the Holy Spirit." In Holy Writ, the Holy Spirit is the thing received: "They had not yet received the Holy Spirit"; "They received the Holy Spirit";[94] "Have you received the Holy Spirit?"[95] St. Peter, explaining why he had received the Gentiles into the Church, said that the Holy Spirit fell upon them as He had on the Apostles on Pentecost day. "If, then, God gave them the same Gift as to us who believed in the Lord Jesus Christ, who was I, that I could withstand God?"

It is also exceedingly likely that the bright cloud that overshadowed our Lord at the Transfiguration must be considered as an emblematic manifestation of the Holy Spirit. Many Fathers, Sts. Augustine, Gregory, Ambrose, Bede, and Bernard, with Origen and Theophylact,[96] are of

---

[94] Acts 8:17.

[95] Acts 19:2.

[96] St. Gregory (d. 604), Pope from 590, writer, and Doctor; St. Bede (672-735), English monk and scholar; St. Bernard of Clairvaux (1090-1153), abbot and Doctor; Origen of Alexandria (185-254), theologian; Theophylact (d. c. 1107), biblical commentator.

this conviction, and are accepted by St. Thomas Aquinas as constituting reliable Patristic tradition. Moreover, on the feast of the Transfiguration, the Church says, "In the bright cloud the Holy Spirit was seen, the voice of the Father was heard: This is my beloved Son."

Dominicans are told to say the Preface *"De Trinitate"* on that day, clearly because the Trinity stood revealed on that day. The account of the Transfiguration in the Gospels and in St. Peter's letter and its parallelism with the account of Christ's baptism support the idea that the bright cloud symbolized the Holy Spirit. St. Luke indicates that the cloud not only overshadowed, but even enveloped them, and that the Apostles were afraid when they entered the cloud. This cloud appeared only when Moses and Elijah had left Jesus, as if to single out our Lord and distinguish Him from His two companions. The overshadowing as by a cloud was certainly a symbol of the divinity in the words of St. Gabriel to our Lady: "The Holy Spirit shall come upon thee, and the power of the Most High shall overshadow thee."

The Holy Spirit proceeds not only from the Father, but from the Father and the Son. In discussing the matter, we must be careful to distinguish between the purely doctrinal question of the revealed truth in itself and the interesting but merely historical question of the insertion of *Filioque* ("and from the Son") in the Nicene-Constantinopolitan Creed.

Any Catholic with any sense of the supremacy and sovereignty of the Church in disciplinary matters concerning her own devotional and liturgical life must acknowledge her right to add any words to the recital of a public creed that express revealed truth. It would be childish to maintain that she who wrote the creeds could not add to them, or that any council or authority whatsoever could bind herself in the choice of words to express truth. If a council forbids addition to a creed, it means additions that qualify, minimize, or explain away the truth enunciated. As a mere disciplinary matter, the Church can forbid any verbal additions to public creeds by unauthorized persons; she can do this owing to the particular dangers attending special circumstances, but, since he who makes the law can alter the law, she could not make a disciplinary law that she herself could not revoke.

As a matter of fact, the creed in question, the so-called Nicene Creed of A.D. 325, was considerably added to in 381 at the Council of Constantinople. Even today the Church still permits the singing or public recital of that creed without the addition of *Filioque* during the Liturgy by Greek Catholics, whose Faith is the same as hers. She thereby shows her sovereignty and absolute freedom in matters of mere discipline.

Questions of doctrine are totally different. There she must insist on absolute unity. Hence, every Catholic must believe that the Holy Spirit proceeds from the Father and the Son. That is taught in holy Scripture. That is taught by the Fathers. That is the Faith of the Catholic Church. Three general councils solemnly taught it: the fourth Council of the Lateran, the second of Lyons, and the Council of Florence. This last council decreed, "From all eternity, the Holy Spirit is from the Father and the Son; He has His essence and His subsistent being from the Father together with the Son; and He proceeds from either eternally as from one principle and by one spiration [breathing out]."

In the Gospel of John we read plainly that Christ said of the Holy Spirit, "He shall not speak of Himself, but whatsoever He shall hear, He shall speak, and the things that are to come, He shall shew you. He shall glorify me, because *He shall receive of mine and shew it to you.* All things whatsoever the Father hath are mine; therefore I said that He shall receive of mine and shew it to you."[97]

[97] John 16:13-15.

Nothing surely could be plainer: the Holy Spirit receives the divinity from the Son, because the Son receives all — that is, the whole divinity — from the Father. The expression likewise, "He shall speak whatsoever He shall hear" is an expression of the reception of the divinity, for Christ had previously said of Himself as the Son, " 'He that sent me is true, and what I have heard from Him, that I speak in the world.' And they did not understand that He called God His Father."[98] Moreover, Christ said, "When the Paraclete shall come whom I shall send you from the Father . . ."[99] No divine Person could be said to be *sent* by another divine Person unless He received the divinity from Him and originated from Him. Hence, the Scriptures call the Holy Spirit the Spirit of Christ as they call Him the Spirit of God.

The Fathers of the Church, the Greek as well as the Latin Fathers, use the same phrases of the relation of Holy Spirit to the Son as they use of His relation to the Father, with the exception, of course, of generation or sonship.

They call the Son the fount and the principle of the Holy Spirit; the Holy Spirit goes forth from Him, flows

[98] John 8:26-27.
[99] John 15:26.

out from Him, is poured out by Him. He belongs to Him; He is of the substance of Him; He is the Son's glory, splendor, light, and fire. St. Epiphanius[100] directly uses the words "The Spirit of the Father and the Spirit of the Son"; "proceeding from the Father and the Son." So also St. Chrysostom:[101] "Christ came to us and gave us the Spirit, who is from Him." Even if St. John Damascene wishes to limit the Greek expression "out of" to the relation of the Holy Spirit to the Father, because it expresses the first fount and principle, the saint agrees that the Holy Spirit proceeded from the Father through the Son, which comes to the same thing.

Even reason illumined by revelation suggests the same truth. Since the three Personalities are constituted by their very relationship as opposites in origin to one another, the Holy Spirit would not be distinct from, but would coincide with the Person of the Son unless He stood to Him as originated to originator.

Moreover, the Son being produced by the intellect of the Father as His Word, and not by the will as object

[100] St. Epiphanius (310-403), Archbishop of Salamis.

[101] St. John Chrysostom (c. 347-407), Archbishop of Constantinople and Doctor; named Chrysostom, meaning "Golden Mouth," for his eloquent preaching.

willed, receives the divine nature as if it were still pregnant with the divine will. The production by *mind* must of necessity precede that by *will*, since nothing can be willed except as known. The Son, therefore, possessing the divine nature containing the divine will not breathed forth, of necessity breathes it out as the Holy Spirit.

When the Council of Florence defines that the Holy Spirit proceeds "as from one principle and by one spiration," it means that although the Father and the Son are two Persons and therefore two Agents, there are not two distinct acts by which the Holy Spirit is produced, but rather, one single, infinite, eternal act common to both Persons.

This act does belong to Either in His own way, to the Father as unoriginated, unborn, or to the Son as received, originated, and generated.

To understand this a little better, we may turn to a comparison with the fact of the creation of the world. The world has not three creators but one; the world proceeds from one Principle, not three principles, for although there are three Persons in the Godhead, toward all that is not God, they act as one single principle, since They act by Their nature, which is one. So one may say that Father and Son act by the divine will, which is one.

Chapter Nine

⚜

Each Person of the Trinity has a mission

We read repeatedly in Holy Scripture that a divine Person is *sent*. "I am not alone," said our Lord, "but I and the Father who sent me."[102]

We read in St. Paul, "God sent the Spirit of His Son into your hearts."[103] Again, our Lord said, "But when I shall have gone, I shall send Him [the Holy Spirit] to you."[104] And of our Lord it stands written, "When the fullness of time had come, God sent His Son into the world."[105]

[102] John 8:16.
[103] Gal. 4:6.
[104] Cf. John 16:7.
[105] Cf. Gal. 4:4.

Understanding the Trinity

What precisely do we mean by this sending? Is it a command that must be obeyed? Is it a request or an impulse from one divine Person to the Other? Can it imply the subjection of one Person to the Other? Besides, all three Persons are omnipresent. What, then, does this sending involve or express?

It expresses the origin of one Person from the Other in the Godhead in relation to some temporal effect in this world. Let us explain. The general meaning of *sending*, the normal idea of a mission involves the motion of one person by another person toward a certain terminus, considered either as place, or as effect or product.

Among rational creatures this sending is done by command or at least counsel. Among divine Persons, who can be neither commanded nor counseled, the notion of sending can be verified only in the procession of one Person from the Other. To speak of a person being sent, that is, moved toward some terminus of place or effect, this person must have *from* another the will to reach that place or to produce that effect. Among us men the will of the messenger or person sent is impelled toward that terminus by another's request or advice, but in God this can only be in that a Person, through the procession of origin, has from another Person the divine nature, and therefore the divine will, which is identical with that nature, to reach that terminus, to go to that place, or to produce that effect. Our blessed Lord explains His own sending by saying, "I went out from the Father and came into the world."[106]

The relation of origin of one Person from the Other within the Godhead would by itself not yet justify the use of the word *sending,* as St. Augustine appositely remarks: "The Son is not said to have been sent on account of the mere fact that He appeared unto this world as the Word made flesh."[107] It is, therefore, a plain consequence that only the Son and the Holy Spirit are "sent." The Father is never sent, the Son sends the Holy Spirit, but the Holy Spirit never sends another Person; the Holy Spirit *comes*.

The one substantial mission is that of the second Person in the Incarnation, for then God the Son was not merely shown by some figure or representation, but He was substantially united to the visible human nature of our Lord.

The sending or outpouring of the Holy Spirit into our hearts by grace, however real, is naturally invisible. Some new external extraordinary sign is required, and this must aim at santification.

[106] Cf. John 16:28.
[107] *De Trin.,* IV.

This mission can be substantial or merely representative — that is, by symbol or representation.

Holy Scripture gives us four missions of the Holy Spirit by symbolic action: at Christ's baptism as a dove, at the Transfiguration as a lightsome cloud, on Easter evening as the breath of our Lord, and on Pentecost day as tongues of fire. On each occasion, the sign was one of sanctification — in the cases of our Lord in the Jordan and on Mount Thabor, of the divine grace bestowed in the Hypostatic Union; in the two other cases, of the divine grace bestowed on men.

One might say by appropriation that there is a perpetual sending, an uninterrupted outpouring of the Holy Spirit on and in the Church of Christ ever since Pentecost. It is this constant sending and consequent indwelling in the Church that maintains it in infallible truth, guarding the Deposit of the Faith and constantly increasing our understanding of it, for the Holy Spirit as Spirit of Father and Son is the Spirit of Truth. It is this conviction that makes the Church recite the *Veni Creator* before coming to grave decisions. One might speak of a perpetual sending of the Holy Spirit into the hearts of men, expressed in the prayer: "Send forth Thy Spirit, and they shall be created, and Thou shalt renew the face of the earth." If this sending by grace is invisible, it is in some sense made visible or at least attached to an outward visible sign in the three sacraments that bestow the Holy Spirit: Baptism, Confirmation, and Holy Orders.

In Scripture and in Christian speech, we find the ascription of special attributes and functions to each of the three Persons. We are all acquainted with the custom of attributing creation to God the Father. The Apostles' Creed begins, "I believe in God, the Father Almighty, Creator of Heaven and earth." We describe God the Son as Redeemer of the world, and the Holy Spirit is invoked as the Sanctifier, the Life-giver of our souls. Since it is of faith that the three Persons have all divine attributes in common and that, in producing any external created effect, they all act together as one, how do we explain this appropriation?

It is nothing else than assigning something that is common to several, to one in particular, as if proper to him. Why is this done in Holy Writ and in normal Christian speech? There must be some lawful reason for and some utility in doing so. The reason cannot be that some attribute or activity belongs to one Person alone, or at least more to Him than to Another. The real reason is a certain similarity between the appropriated attribute or activity and the special characteristic of the personality to whom it is appropriated.

Examples will show what is meant. The proper characteristic of the Father is to be the originating principle in the Trinity, and it is easy to see that there is a certain affinity between this and creation, between this and omnipotence. For creating means being the principle and origin of things outside oneself; and omnipotence appears to us as the principle through which things are produced.

The most frequent designation of God the Father in the Liturgy is "Almighty, eternal God." In this eternity is joined to omnipotence. Beginning-less or eternal existence suggests to us the fact that the Father is the First in origin within the Trinity, although, of course, not in time, since there is no time in God. It is an echo of the Scriptural phrase applied to God the Father as "the Ancient of days,"[108] and it is embodied in art when the Father is portrayed with the white-haired venerable aspect of an old man. We have already pointed out elsewhere that the Scriptures, so to say, appropriate the term *God* to God the Father, not that He is more God than the two other Persons, but because in the order of timeless origin the

[108] Dan. 7:9.

Godhead begins with Him, and He has it as His own and unreceived while bestowing it on Others.

To the Son as hypostatic knowledge of the Father is appropriated the attribute of divine wisdom and all external works inasmuch as they are considered as expressions of wisdom. Therefore we attribute to the Son the wise disposition of things in the universe, and especially the work of our redemption, which is the restitution of the divine order disturbed by our sins.

When we pray, "God the Son, Redeemer of the world, have mercy on us," we thereby remind ourselves of two things: first, that God the Son alone has assumed to Himself the human nature that was God's instrument in our redemption, and, second, that our redemption as the restoration of ourselves and all the world to pristine integrity is the highest manifestation of divine wisdom, and therefore reveals to us the Word as the wisdom of the Father.

To the Holy Spirit we appropriate, as God's love in person, the attributes of goodness and charity and the external works as manifestation of divine bounty, and, therefore, most of all, the work of our sanctification, since the bestowal of grace and holiness shows us the characteristic of the third Person as spirit of holiness.

According to St. Paul, all created things are by appropriation said to be *from* the Father, *through* the Son, *into* the Holy Spirit.[109] From Him, through Him, and into Him are all things.

The preposition *from* indicates the source and acting cause. This is appropriated to the Father to whom, as origin and fount, all power is attributed; hence, all creatures are from the Father. *Through* indicates the way in which an agent proceeds to work as we say an artist works by or through his art. God acts through His wisdom, but the Son is the personal wisdom of the Father; hence, He is said to act *through* the Son. *Into* means the attitude toward the final end to which all things tend and in which they rest. God is the final end because He is the ultimate good, but goodness is appropriated to the third Person; hence, He is also the ultimate end. Thus, all things are from the Father, through the Son, into the Holy Spirit.

We are warned in Holy Scripture not to *grieve* the Holy Spirit.[110] To grieve means to cause sorrow *to a friend*. Through grace we become friends of God, and this friendship is by appropriation attributed to the Holy Spirit,

[109]Cf. Rom. 11:36.
[110]Eph. 4:30.

since friendship is a manifestation of special kindness and goodness of a well-wisher to another.

The Holy Spirit is the subsistent will, love, and bounty of God. Hence also is He the Paraclete, the Comforter, who by the tenderness of His intimacy performs the functions of a friend in soothing the distress of one He loves.

The workings of grace within our soul are likewise appropriated to the Holy Spirit for the same reason. "The Spirit Himself giveth testimony to our spirit that we are the sons of God."[111] "The Spirit helpeth our infirmity, for we know not what we should pray for as we ought, but the Spirit Himself asketh for us with ineffable groanings, and He that searcheth the hearts knoweth what the Spirit desireth, because He asketh for the saints according to God."[112]

In these texts, what we ourselves do under the influence of divine grace is attributed to the Holy Spirit as the Author of grace. Being in His Person the outcome of the will of Father and Son, the supreme gift of God to man, divine grace is attributed to Him, and He is even said to do within us what we do by His grace.

[111] Rom. 8:16.
[112] Rom. 8:26-27.

Understanding the Trinity

There were once some devout persons in the Catholic Church who thought it strange that there should be so many solemn feast days in honor of our blessed Lord, the second Person in the Trinity, that one of the greatest solemnities was Pentecost, dedicated to the third Person, but that the first Person, God the Father, should be without any feast day at all during the year's cycle. They tried to induce Rome to authorize a feast of God the Father. Leo XIII answered with precision and clarity: "Our predecessor Innocent XII (A.D. 1700) when asked for some solemnities proper to God the Father, absolutely refused. Although the separate mysteries of the Incarnate Word are celebrated on certain feast days, yet the Word according to His divine nature alone is not celebrated by any proper feast; and even the solemnities of Pentecost were not introduced of old for the purpose that the Holy Spirit by Himself as such should be honored but that His coming or external mission should be commemorated. These things were indeed thus sanctioned by wise counsel lest anyone perchance from distinguishing the divine Persons should proceed falsely to distinguishing the divine essence."

Chapter Ten

✲

The Trinity dwells in you

From Holy Scripture it is clear that there is a special in-dwelling of God in the souls of the just. "If anyone love me, he will keep my word, and my Father will love him, and we shall come to him and take up our abode with him."[113] "You shall know that I am in the Father, and you in me and I in you."[114] "Abide in me. . . . He that abideth in me and I in him, he shall bear fruit."[115] "I shall ask the Father, and He shall give you another Paraclete, that He abide with you forever. He shall remain with you and shall be in you."[116]

[113] Cf. John 14:23.
[114] John 14:20.
[115] Cf. John 15:4-5.
[116] Cf. John 14:16-17.

St. John in his first letter writes, "If we love one another, God remaineth in us. We shall remain in Him and He in us. He who remains in charity, remaineth in God and God in him."[117] The same truth is emphasized by St. Paul: "Christ liveth in me."[118] "If Christ is in you . . ."[119] "I bend my knees to the Father . . . that He give you that Christ dwell through faith in your hearts."[120] "Because you are sons, God has sent the spirit of His Son into your hearts crying, 'Abba, Father.' "[121] "The Spirit of God dwelleth in him. But if anyone have not the Spirit of Christ, he is none of his."[122] "Know ye not that you are the temples of God and that the Spirit of God dwelleth in you?"[123] "You are the temple of the living God."[124]

What precisely do we mean by this presence of God within us? On first thought, it might seem that God could

[117]Cf. 1 John 4:12, 16.
[118]Gal. 2:20.
[119]Cf. Rom. 8:10.
[120]Cf. Eph. 3:14, 16.
[121]Gal. 4:6.
[122]Cf. Rom. 8:9.
[123]1 Cor. 3:16.
[124]2 Cor. 6:16.

not possibly come nearer to us, and be more intimate to us, more within us than He must always of necessity be. God is everywhere and cannot be absent anywhere in this creation.

Philosophy tells us that God is everywhere in a threefold way: *per essentiam*, *per potentiam*, and *per presentiam*. This means, first, that He is everywhere by His very being and essence, for created things are only reflections, analogies of Him; they exist because He exists, as a portrait in a mirror exists because of the person who stands before it. It means that He is in all things by His power, since they are what He wills them to be and *because* He wills them to be. It means, thirdly, that they are present unto Him as utterly known to Him. Corporeal presence is to be within the compass of one or more of our senses; presence spiritual or intellectual is presence to our mind, perceptible and perceived by our understanding.

Hence, God is not present to us as we are to Him; we are present to Him absolutely, but He is present to us only in the measure that we know Him. We cannot know Him by our senses. We can know Him only by our mind. In that sense, He is present to every human mind, except for a short time to some diseased minds who might doubt or deny His existence. God then renders Himself present to us by maintaining our human reason through which we become aware of the fact *that* He is, and, by analogy, also of *what* He is.

Moreover, as God is naturally known as the supreme and infinite Good, man's will naturally reaches out to God to be united to Him and to possess Him. This knowledge may be indirect and faint, this human will may be feeble and distraught, but radically it is always there.

This may be called the natural indwelling of God in the soul of man. But there is a supernatural indwelling that is due to supernatural grace.

This supernatural indwelling is of the same kind as the natural indwelling in that it affects the mind and the will, the two constituent factors in the life of the soul. Revealed by faith, made attainable through hope and enjoyed and embraced by charity, God becomes intimately present to the soul in a way that exceeds all the powers of nature.

Let us, however, not be mistaken and think that this intimate supernatural presence of God within the soul consists itself in the human acts we make toward Him. These acts are the result of the divine presence; they are not that presence itself. This presence consists in that God so holds the soul, pervades the soul, and lives within the substance of the soul that He offers Himself as object to the soul's powers of knowledge and will. He makes Himself knowable and lovable by operating on the innermost fibers of our being and drawing us toward Himself as the divine object to be understood, striven for, and possessed. This divine presence is not our act of knowledge and love as such; otherwise it would not be in the baptized infant before he reaches the age of reason or the adult person who is asleep or forgetful of God for a while, but it is God Himself causing such a condition of the human soul that, on exercising its faculties, the soul finds God within itself as the term, end, and object of its powers of mind and will.

Let us recall that God is not one Person, but three Persons. Hence, all three Persons, Father, Son, and Holy Spirit, thus dwell within us. Since each Person is infinitely distinct from the Others, they dwell within us such as in fact they are: the Father, the source and wellspring of the Godhead; the Son, eternally begotten from the Father, the splendor of His glory, the Word eternally uttered; the Holy Spirit proceeding from Father and Son and their subsistent love. It is not that their mode of presence varies as if any of the Three were more or less present than the Others, or present in another way, for all actions of God outward, all actions toward His creatures are of necessity equally the work of all Three. Their mode of presence is the same, but *They* are not the same; the person of the Father is not that of the Son, and so on.

Three Persons dwell in us, Each as He is in fact in the divine drama of Their eternal relationship, this relationship of each One to the Others is a reality *within us*. Each Person by ineffable intimacy touches our soul and is in contact with it.

Scripture seems to ascribe some special indwelling in our soul to the Holy Spirit, but this ascription does not mean that the Holy Spirit does something different in us from what the Others do — this would be impossible — but that He is within us in His distinct personality: the subsisting love and holiness, the fulfillment or complementum of the Trinity. Hence, He is the supreme gift of God to us, the love of God to us, since He is holiness as person. By dwelling in us, He makes our soul a temple, a sanctuary. Since He proceeds from Father and Son, the highest truth and light of intelligence, He is within us as illuminating the very depth of our soul.

When we pray, "Come, Holy Spirit," we do not ask for a presence of the third Person in any way apart from the Others and special to Him alone. This would be a sheer impossibility, for the Holy Spirit can "come" only by being breathed forth by the Father and the Son. Hence, They give Him to us, and for as much as He is given by Them, He comes to us. In our prayers, therefore, we naturally beg that the Father and the Son might give and that the Spirit might come. He is indeed a gift, but a living gift, a Person, who when being bestowed is coming to us.

All whatsoever is done in our souls is always done by or from the Father through the Son in the Holy Spirit. One reads sometimes that through grace we stand in a special relation to the Holy Spirit. Such expressions should not be misunderstood as if there were a bond between us and the third Person that did not exist between us and the other Two. Our soul is related to, linked with, God, but God is three Persons. Hence, we can speak of a threefold link or relation only in the sense that there are Three to whom we are linked, and these Three are related between Themselves by eternal begetting, eternal being born, and eternal proceeding or being breathed forth. We are not linked to the Godhead in the abstract or the divine nature, for there is no abstract divine nature. Divine nature is numerically one; it is God, and God is the Blessed Trinity. Hence, our Lord says so beautifully and tenderly, "If anyone love me, my Father will love him and we shall come and take our abode with him."

Chapter Eleven

ِ٭

You shall behold
the Trinity in Heaven

Shall we ever understand the mystery of the Blessed Trinity, or will it forever be shrouded in darkness or twilight even in eternity? Since God is infinite and our mind remains finite even in Heaven, must we conclude that we shall never really and fully understand that God is Father, Son, and Holy Spirit? Will our act of adoration in everlasting life always be an act of humble submission of mind, an act of mental obedience in which we accept a truth because God said so, and not because we see it ourselves?

We shall happily see it for ourselves. There is no faith in Heaven. We shall know and no longer believe. Faith and hope shall pass away. Only charity shall remain. In love we shall adore the Three: Father, Son, and Holy Spirit.

It is indeed perfectly true that our minds are finite and that God is infinite, and therefore the finite will never encompass or mentally comprehend and completely embrace all that is knowable of God. Were we, on an impossible supposition, to do so, we would be God ourselves, for we would possess an infinite mind.

But it is also true that God has promised that we should see Him face-to-face, see Him even as He is, know Him even as we are known.[125] "No one knoweth the Son but the Father, and no one knoweth the Father but the Son": so runs the text, but the text goes on: "and he to whom it shall please the Son to reveal Him."[126]

There are therefore some who know already, or are destined to know, the Father and the Son after some fashion comparable to that in which They know one another. Comparable, I say, as far as creatures in their activity can be likened to the activity of God. God has promised that we should see Him face-to-face; that means a closeness, a directness, an immediacy of knowledge that can only be portrayed symbolically by the mutual gaze of two persons, who look one another in the eyes.

[125] 1 Cor. 13:12.
[126] Matt. 11:27.

You shall behold the Trinity in Heaven

During our life on earth, we only know about God. After this life we shall know no longer by inference or by hearsay; neither arguments, nor efforts of faith or reason shall be required, for there shall be the obviousness of sight itself, sight not indeed of bodily eyes, but a higher sight that acts by intellectual light.

The Church has found a name for this new supernatural light of intelligence. She styles it "the light of glory," *lumen gloriae*. This light dispenses with laborious steps of logic by which we now prove that God exists. It surpasses that certitude by which we believe because God has spoken. It is more like our awareness of the sun shining in our eyes at noonday from a cloudless sky.

All our present earthly knowledge is by images, ideas, concepts that intervene between us and the thing in itself that we see, perceive, or know. Our cognitive faculty apprehends indeed its object in some way, yet the object always remains outside it. The substance of my soul and the substance of the thing I know are not in immediate contact. The thing itself does not pervade me, hold me, enter into me. I only gaze at reality as over against me, as a man might look at a picture.

In Heaven this will be different. God will not be a picture to be gazed at or admired at a distance. God will give

Himself to me to be known. I shall know Him because I shall be united to Him. God shall enter into me and I into Him. God shall dwell in me, as the fire of the furnace dwells within the bar of metal that lies molten within its glow.

We have seen that already during this life God is intimately present to us since He is close to us by His power, by His knowledge, and by His very essence. We have seen that, if we are in the state of grace, God supernaturally dwells within us, and each Person of the Godhead as He is: the Father, the Son, and the Holy Spirit. What, then, can Heaven add to the intimacy of this presence?

It adds this: on earth we have no immediate constant consciousness of this indwelling. We know by reason and by faith that it must be so, but it is a mere conclusion of our abstract reason, and in the case of our faith. It is backed and supported by our will moved by divine grace. It is a bare logical process all the same, although raised to the supernatural plane, a chain of premises leading to the final act of faith.

In Heaven it will be a vital direct awareness, an immediate perception by which we apprehend God within us, by which we perpetually behold God as He is: God the Father, the Son, and the Holy Spirit. We shall be as a diamond laid in the sun, pellucid in its rays, and we shall know it uninterruptedly throughout all eternity. Or, rather, we should not compare it to a lifeless thing. It will be what Christ called it: everlasting life, that is, life with and in the eternal God; with and in the Father, the Son, and the Holy Spirit.

To our intellect at present, the divine nature appears as something formally distinct from the three divine Persons. We now speak of the Godhead, the Divinity, as something abstract, as we speak of manhood or humanity. In reality there is no abstraction corresponding to the divine nature as separate from the three Persons; there are only the three Persons, and these three are the one God. Hence, to see God is to see three Persons. It is to utter the threefold *Sanctus* to the singleness of God.

In Heaven we shall be in the bosom of the Father, heirs by adoption of the glory of the only-begotten Son, knowing that we are sanctified utterly and forever by the indwelling of the Holy Spirit. Unto God the Father we shall cry, "Abba: Father," echoing the cry of the human nature of Christ our Lord. Unto the only-begotten One we shall say, "Divine Brother, we are Thine by adoption." The Holy Spirit we shall embrace as Him who has chosen our heart as His temple, for we have become a conscious sanctuary of the All-Holy One; our whole being is a shrine of the triune God.

The blessed in Heaven do not contemplate some abstract divinity. They do not philosophize or discuss some idea of the beautiful, the good, and the true. Without any discursive reasonings whatever, their mind is riveted, their will irresistibly drawn; their whole being is blissfully captive in the embrace of the Father, the Son, and the Holy Spirit.

Sometimes, so it seems, God gives a faint foretaste of that heavenly bliss to His saints during their life on earth. It is generally held that the Beatific Vision itself is never bestowed on men during their mortal life, however saintly they may be, but there appears to be a marvelous, although lesser gift that can be received even while the soul is still in the body.

This seems to consist in some intuitional awareness of God's presence, which transcends all processes of reasoning and is some immediate intellectual experience, which cannot be described in the formulas of philosophy and is beyond human words to utter. A number of saints have claimed that in this sublime experience they became aware of the triplicity of persons in God, and the mystery of the Trinity lay in some sense unveiled before them. The bulk of the faithful to whom such high ecstasy is not given are nonetheless comforted by the sure hope that for them also the Blessed Trinity shall one day be a mystery no longer, but an open secret to enjoy.

Perhaps we should not have written "open secret," for it will cease to be a secret in any sense except in the remembrance that formerly, during their short sojourn on earth, it was not known. A secret is a truth a man knows that he could understand, but does not. A secret implies a lack of understanding, which leaves man's craving for knowledge unsatisfied. But the mind of the blessed shall be satiated, each in his own measure, to the utmost of his capacity in the eternal light that floods his soul — the light that streams from the throne of the Ancient One of days, and His only-begotten One, and the Spirit of love who proceeds from Them both. The time for search or question is over. Nothing remains for the blessed but the joy of praise: Glory be to the Father and to the Son and to the Holy Spirit. As it was in the beginning, is now, and ever shall be world without end.

Appendix

༈

Chapter Twelve

The Trinity in ancient philosophy

It has been maintained that the Christian doctrine was the natural outcome of the philosophical speculations current at the time of the origin of Christianity. This is historically untenable. It is of the essence of the Trinity that there should be three Persons in God and not Two to which a Third is casually added.

Now there existed no contemporary speculation concerning a threefoldness within the Godhead. The Holy Spirit is not an afterthought in Christian revelation. The Founder of Christianity spoke of Him before He died. St. Peter spoke of Him when the first converts were made. In fact, Christianity as an organized movement after the Ascension of its Founder began precisely by the visible outpouring of the Holy Spirit.

Understanding the Trinity

The Holy Trinity is not the slow fruit of speculation on existing Jewish or pagan ideas. It was revealed by the Founder out of the plenitude of His knowledge. To paint the Founder as a philosopher, a theorizer with other people's opinions, is not to write history, but to indulge in fancies contradicted by the early documents of Christianity: the Gospel, the Acts, and the letters of its first apostles.

There is no record among Jew or Gentile of that time of a speculation of a Spirit as a person within God, and distinct from the emanation of His Son or Word. If such a record were found, it would still be necessary to show that this speculation influenced Christ and His Apostles.

We admit that there existed indeed a speculation concerning the *Logos*, the Word of God. There was a Jewish philosopher, born at Alexandria some twenty years before our Lord, whose name was Philo. He employed the Greek term *Logos*, which had already been used some centuries before by Stoic philosophers, as the divine reason manifested in the organization of the universe.

Philo adapted the idea to include Plato's theory that this visible world had an invisible replica in the thought-world beyond. In a confused rhetorical way, he sometimes personifies this *Logos*, or Word, but it is never clear whether it is the Stoic *Logos* or the Platonist *Logos*, or an amalgam of both that he means. In any case, this *Logos* is not even certainly distinct from the Godhead, and if distinct, it is certainly not divine, but a creature. Even though, as a literary device, Philo sometimes calls the *Logos* God, he explains that he is not God in the real sense. To Philo a duality or triplicity of persons within the Godhead would be absolutely repellent. Jewry was from the first the fiercest opponent of Christianity, precisely because they regarded the Christians as blasphemers who denied the unity of the Godhead. True, there are in the Old Testament a number of indications, suggestions, and adumbrations of the mystery of the Trinity, but the Christian revelation is not properly a human development of these remote faint hints.

Without Christ's direct plain statements, no one could possibly have concluded to a divine trinity from them. The proof of this lies in the historical fact that the bulk of those who acknowledged the Old Testament as divinely inspired Scripture not only did not do so, but fiercely attacked those who did, and they have remained their most absolute opponents even until today.

Some non-Catholic scholars will have it that the doctrine of the Blessed Trinity, although not born directly from Philo's Jewish speculations, was yet the fruit of a combination of Jewish and pagan speculations in the Gnostic schools of the first century. These learned men cannot see the forest for the trees. It is quite true that the first two or three centuries are full of the weirdest speculations of so-called religious intellectuals who styled themselves Gnostics, that is, "people who know," for *gnosis* is the Greek word for "knowledge."

It is quite true also that in their later speculations after the rise of Christianity, they even found a place in their complicated systems for an emanation from the deity called the Holy Spirit, but resemblance of words is not always a proof of resemblance of ideas. All Gnostic theories, of whatever kind, have a completely different aim from that of Christian Trinitarian dogma. Gnostics tried to explain that where matter was, there was evil, for matter was evil, spirit was good. Gnostics are only Hellenized Manicheans. For them the problem to be solved was how a good spiritual God was connected with this evil world. Their fancy conjured up a series, sometimes a score, of intermediate semidivine, semimaterialized beings emanating from the supreme God and making a link with this gross sinful world. Each of these imagined emanations from the all-holy God was a little less spiritual, immaterial, holy, and inaccessible than his immediate predecessor.

In this way, a chain was established by which the first or highest God, utterly spiritual, ineffable, and unapproachable, could come into contact with this universe, and the transcendant could reach the particular and the concrete.

The Christian Trinity has nothing whatever to do with an explanation of the origin of matter or of evil. It tells us something of God as such. It does not want to make a bridge between God and His creatures. God the Son and God the Holy Spirit are not nearer to creature status than God the Father Himself. Gnostics professed to know nothing whatever of God in His pure divine nature. They invented their rather childish hierarchy of emanations for the express purpose of bringing home to people that God in Himself was completely unknown. He was "the Depth," "the Invisible," "the Inaccessible"; direct contact between Him and creatures was essentially impossible. They might sometimes style him Father and give him a son, they might establish a score of angel-spirits between Him and matter, and even call one of them "the Holy Spirit," but the fact remains that these beings were either just creatures or they were a disguise for pantheism.

The Christian Trinity was, unlike Gnosticism, not the fruit of any speculation at all. It was not the result of any theory; it was the result of observation and actual experience. The Apostles had personally come in contact with a Person who, although human by nature, claimed to be God in act and word, and since He proved His claim by rising from the dead, they accepted His claim. Since, however, He distinguished between Himself and God His Father, there were two Persons in God: the Father and the Son. Again, their divine Christ had promised before His death to send another divine Person, who, as He said, proceeded from the Father and received from the Son. This Person had come in a miraculous manner in flames of fire resting on their heads. Hence, there were clearly three divine Persons, and, obeying the command of their divine Master, the Apostles had baptized the new converts into the one Name of these three Persons in God.

After they thus baptized them, this third Person manifested Himself by signs and wonders to these new members of the Church of Christ. That is the historical origin of the doctrine of the Blessed Trinity and not philosophical theories of simple fishermen and of the first simple Jews and Gentiles, who first accepted the new Faith.

Chapter Thirteen

꙰

The Trinity and modern errors

An Austrian Catholic priest, Antony Guenther by name, who lived and worked in Vienna for forty years and died there in 1863, entered into all sorts of speculations in the field of theology. He was a man of noble purpose and great industry and wished to vindicate Catholic dogmas purely by reason.

His attempt to do so in the case of the blessed Trinity led him into strange errors. He confused consciousness with personality and defined a person as "a self-conscious nature," and thus brought three self-conscious natures into the Trinity. Although these Persons represented the three factors of the process of divine consciousness, they formed one absolute consciousness or person by what he called a "qualitative" unity, which was neither numerically nor specifically one.

Understanding the Trinity

Now, a person is indeed a distinct subsistency in an intellectual nature, and self-consciousness is an activity of an intellectual nature since it is an act of knowledge, but a person is not essentially constituted by this knowledge. There are not three knowledges and wills in God. Each Person knows and wills with the numerically one mind and will of God. Rome, while praising Guenther's good intentions, condemned his theories, and he duly submitted.

In modern days, a vast number of those who by official position or clerical profession are held to accept the faith in the blessed Trinity, are in reality Unitarians, each one having some way of his own of reconciling the ancient formulas of Christianity with a denial of their historical meaning. Obviously, as faith in the Godhead of Christ, the true faith in the Incarnation, recedes, belief in the Trinity becomes an impossibility. Outside the Catholic Church, in what was once "the Protestant world," belief in Jesus as God is dwindling so fast that it is impossible to say what still remains. Perhaps it lingers on to some extent in the minds of the laity, especially the unsophisticated, to whom the refrain of the doxology after psalms and hymns has still some value; but among higher clergy, it is hard to say how much is still believed. The extreme aversion from the use of the Athanasian Creed is a bad sign.

The Trinity and modern errors

A quaint perversion of Trinitarian belief appeared in the philosophy of Hegel. It is the insertion of Christian phraseology into idealistic pantheism.

Professor Muirhead excellently sums this up in his article on Hegel in the *Encyclopaedia Britannica* (in the Evolution of Religion):

> We pass to those faiths where the Godhead takes the form of a spiritual individuality, i.e., to the Hebrew religion (of sublimity), the Greek (of beauty), and the Roman (of adaptation). Last comes absolute religion in which the mystery of the reconciliation between God and man is an open doctrine. This is Christianity in which God is a Trinity, because He is a spirit. The revelation of this truth is the subject of the Christian Scriptures. For the Son of God, in the immediate aspect, is the finite world of nature and man, which far from being at one with its Father is originally in an attitude of estrangement. The history of Christ is the visible reconciliation between man and the eternal. With the death of Christ this union, ceasing to be a mere fact, becomes a vital idea — the Spirit of God which dwells in the Christian community.

Understanding the Trinity

Strange to say, Hegelianism has had and, still has, a fascination, a kind of pietistic charm for Englishmen. Edward Caird wrote:

> The idea of an absolute Unity, which transcends all the oppositions of finitude and especially the last opposition which includes all others — the opposition of subject and object — is the ultimate presupposition of our consciousness. Hence we cannot understand the real character of our rational life or appreciate the full compass of its movement unless we recognize as its necessary constituents or guiding ideas: opposition of subject and object but also the idea of God. The idea of God therefore — meaning by that in the first instance only the idea of an absolute principle of unity which binds in one all thinking beings and all objects of thought, which is at once the source of being to all things that know — is the ultimate essential principle of our intelligence. Every rational being as such is a religious being.

Caird is here struggling with the problem of the seemingly necessary and eternal opposition and duality of Thinker and Object of thought, and yet that there must be some higher principle which is such that it is the source of both or a unity uniting both. He gropes after the truth of the Trinity and yet does not reach it, for he involves this created universe in this transcendent process, whereas it is not a part of it, but a mere finite analogy. This universe is not the Trinity, although Father, Son, and Spirit have left a vestige of themselves in all They have made. Unless we break the spell of pantheism and recognize God as infinitely beyond this world in His nature, although He is within it by power, presence, and essence, and unless we receive the Trinity as God revealed it in the Deity itself, we shall forever be tormented by the problem of the One and the Many, the Thinker and His Thought, the Willer and the Object willed.

Hegelianism of sorts makes its surprising appearance in modern Protestant religious writers even of the "Catholic school."

Canon Peter Green imagines the *Logos*, the Word, the second Person of the Trinity to be the *anima mundi* — the "World-Soul," and Dr. N.P. Williams imagines that Original Sin can be explained by a precosmic fall or deflection of the *Logos*, the Word-Soul! Such writers strongly resent the accusation of pantheism and maintain that they make not God but the *Logos* the World-Soul, but thereby they betray that their Trinity is not the Christian, but the Hegelian one.

Dr. McTaggart, the modern champion of Hegelianism, strenuously maintains that the Ultimate, the Godhead, cannot be personal at all, and on Hegelian principles this is obviously so. It is regrettable that Christian ministers should beguile themselves and beguile others with a phantom Trinity and piously use the terms God, Word, and Spirit when these words have lost all historical meaning and have no connection with the teaching of Christ and His Apostles.

Chapter Fourteen

࣭

Pagan trinities

The doctrine of the Trinity is often contemptuously set aside as merely a variant of philosophical speculations that are found in many religions and really of not more importance than the Brahma, Siva, and Vishnu of the Indians. Now, this statement, however confidently made, is not supported by the evidence of facts. Modern Hindu speculation has indeed evolved a set of three gods, Brahma, Siva, and Vishnu, which we shall discuss presently, but the formation of triads of gods in ancient religions is remarkably rare.

As soon as the deity was degraded to quasihuman status, we find, of course, gods male and gods female and their progeny, and thus sets of gods: father, mother, and son. But this introduction of sex life into the divinity has clearly nothing in common with the Christian Trinity, which is asexual and purely spiritual; moreover, the third Person is not generated from two independent individuals as the fruit of their union. In the Trinity there is but one single personal source and principle, one unborn, unproceeding Person from whom the other Two arise, namely, God the Father. Moreover, in the Trinity the three Persons are co-equal and co-eternal, and all Three possess the one, numerically one, divine nature. The Christian Trinity is the most emphatic assertion of the unity and unicity of the Godhead, whereas in pagan religions, whatever their triad may be, it is an absolute denial of the unity of the Godhead.

In the Egyptian religion, we may have the worship of the material sun, Ra, and this sun may be worshiped as the sun at rising, the sun at noon, and the sun at setting. But this can hardly be adduced as a variant of the Trinity, as it is no speculation at all concerning the nature of the deity, but merely the outcome of observing the visible phases of the material sun in the sky.

In the Egyptian religion, we have, furthermore, the myth of Osiris, Isis, and Horus. Osiris is treacherously slain by his rival Set and descends to the netherworld to become god of the dead. Isis, his sister-wife, mourns him and posthumously gives birth to Horus, who is the triumphant sun, avenging his father. This myth may contain a reminiscence of some remote historical occurrence, or it may be originally some naive dramatization of the sun slain at night by darkness and rising to another, new life in the morning, or most probably, Set is the invading destructive desert overcoming the agricultural strip along the Nile and yet being overcome by the triumph of the new season in the arable land. But whatever be the origin of the tale, how can the Christian Trinity be considered a variant of it? What have they in common beyond the bare number three?

In the Semitic Pantheon, there are multitudinous gods and goddesses, who have children. In the Babylonian religion, as well as the Egyptian one, we know how the city gods or tribal deities, through political changes, the triumph, defeat, or amalgamation of local communities, were thus made relatives to one another for state reasons, and divine genealogies were constructed to meet political needs. But here again, is it not an outrage on common sense to see in these variations of the Christian Trinity?

In the Babylonian Pantheon, the most multitudinous crowd of deities known to history, there is some sort of chief triad of gods: Anu, Bel, and Ea, representing heaven, earth, and sea. The Babylonian Pantheon is an amalgam of Semitic and Sumerian ideas, and the supremacy of a deity depends on the political predominance of the city where he is worshiped.

The gods Anu and Ea are originally Sumerian gods. Ea was the god of the city of Eridu on the Persian Gulf and re-putedly the giver of learning and wisdom. He was the Neptune, or Ocean-god, and embodied the mysterious-ness of the distant waters. Bel is the well-known Baal, or "Lord" of the Bible, since the Semites conceived the deity as lord, or king: *melek*. As "Lord" of the city of Nippur, he took the characteristics of its old Sumerian city god Enlil, a storm-god wielding the hurricane, and was gradually transmuted into the lord of the earth and the lord of man-kind. Anu was the most ancient of all the gods. The word means "heaven" and no doubt was once used for a purer concept of the deity, before it was degraded to a kind of political polytheism. Anu became a shadowy deity, al-though his name usually remained at the head of lists of gods, or at least other gods were identified with him.

Anu-hood was as much as deity, in faint remembrance that Anu was once not a god, but God. When Marduk, the city god of Babylon, and Assur, the city god of the cap-ital of Assyria, gained political supremacy, the statesmen-theologians of the time were accommodating enough to know of a transference of divine power from Anu to their favorite deity. The relationship, however, of Anu, Bel, and Ea was never thought to be that of father and son, or imply any descendance of one god from another. How can anyone of common sense see any connection whatever between their crude Babylonian fancies and the Christian Trinity? One might as well cite Jupiter, Mars, and Mercury or Zeus, Ares, and Hermes as prototypes of God the Father, the Son, and the Holy Spirit.

As the palmary instance of non-Christian Trinity, the Hindu Trimurti of Brahma, Siva, and Vishnu is always brought forward.

The Hindu Trimurti is a late speculation; it does not belong to the ancient Indian or Aryan religion. It came about this way: the worshipers of Vishnu and Siva formed two rival sects. In the original Aryan Pantheon, they were but two lesser deities, but they gradually gained great popularity. Vishnu was a kind, benevolent god; Siva, a stormy and destructive god. Either sect would exalt the greatness of its own god to a sort of identification with absolute deity. This absolute deity was first considered as something impersonal, "Brahma," but in Vishnu "absolute thought and goodness" became more clearly personified and worshiped, not as a faint abstraction, but as an individual.

Understanding the Trinity

Thus Vishnu gives to Brahma personality, and Brahma gives to Vishnu absoluteness and supremacy. To include all three names, the following doctrine was started: Vishnu, that is, Brahma as person, appears as Brahma in order to create the world, as Vishnu (a subordinate form of the original Vishnu) in order to preserve the world, and as Siva in order to destroy it. Thus, the three principles governing this material universe are personified; the productive, or maintaining, and the destructive forces of nature are deified.

It is obvious to all that this Trimurti has nothing in common with the Christian Trinity. It has, in fact, not even the number three strictly in common, since under the three names, Brahma, Vishnu, and Siva, really four realities are pictured, whether we duplicate Brahma, first as the absolute and then as the personal god in Vishnu, or whether we again duplicate Vishnu as representative of Brahma with Vishnu as the maintainer. Moreover, the three gods, Brahma, Vishnu, and Siva, in no sense stand toward one another as the Three in the Christian Trinity: Father, Son, and Holy Spirit.

There is no "destroyer" in the Blessed Trinity, and there is no "Son" in the Hindu Trimurti. In fact, the Trimurti is only a clerical device by which the names of three popular Hindu divinities are attached to the perpetual cosmic process of production, maintenance, and destruction. It is pantheism in the guise of polytheism, and never transcends the material, for even Brahma has a body of some sort and is not pure mind or deity.

Biographical Note

✻

J. P Arendzen

(1873-1954)

John Peter Arendzen studied with the Christian Brothers
in his native Amsterdam and later at Hageveld College in
Leyden, at St. Thomas's Seminary in Hammersmith, London, at the Universities of Bonn and Munich, and at
Christ's College in Cambridge, England. He was ordained
a priest in 1895.

During his studies at Cambridge, he was assigned to St.
Ives parish as a member of the Catholic Missionary Soci-
ety, founded by Cardinal Vaughan in 1902. He taught at
St. Edmund's College in Ware until 1949 and spent his remaining years in Kilburn, North London.

The eloquence and clarity that earned him a place in
the *Daily Mail*'s "Preachers of the Century" is reflected in
his writings, which include books, such as *Prophets*, *Priests*,

and Publicans and *Purgatory and Heaven*, essays, annotations in the Douay Bible, and entries in the Catholic Encyclopedia. Fr. Arendzen's strong, clear explanations of the Faith challenge, equip, and motivate today's readers to continue his missionary work of spreading the gospel in our increasingly secular world.

༺

Sophia Institute Press®

Sophia Institute® is a nonprofit institution that seeks to restore man's knowledge of eternal truth, including man's knowledge of his own nature, his relation to other persons, and his relation to God. Sophia Institute Press® serves this end in numerous ways: it publishes translations of foreign works to make them accessible to English-speaking readers; it brings out-of-print books back into print; and it publishes important new books that fulfill the ideals of Sophia Institute®.

These books afford readers a rich source of the enduring wisdom of mankind. Sophia Institute Press® makes these high-quality books available to the public by using advanced technology and by soliciting donations to subsidize its publishing costs. Your generosity can help Sophia Institute Press® to provide the public with editions of works containing the enduring wisdom of the ages. Please send your tax-deductible contribution to the address below. We also welcome your questions, comments, and suggestions.

For your free catalog, call:
Toll-free: 1-800-888-9344

or write:
Sophia Institute Press®
Box 5284
Manchester, NH 03108

or visit our website:
www.sophiainstitute.com

Sophia Institute® is a tax-exempt institution
as defined by the Internal Revenue Code,
Section 501(c)(3). Tax I.D. 22-2548708.